AS Level
General Studies

Culture, Morality, Arts and Humanities

AQA

AS Level
General Studies

Culture,
Morality, Arts and Humanities

John Barnes
Shaun Best
Rob Dransfield

Published in 2003 by:
Nelson Thornes Ltd
Delta Place
27 Bath Road
CHELTENHAM
GL53 7TH
United Kingdom

03 04 05 06 07 / 10 9 8 7 6 5 4 3 2 1

A catalogue record for this book is available from the British Library

ISBN 0 7487 7120 4

Illustrations by Oxford Designers and Illustrators and Angela Lumley

Page make-up by Northern Phototypesetting Co Ltd, Bolton

Printed and bound in Italy by Canale

contents

dedication   vii

acknowledgements   viii

introduction   xi

chapter 1
An introduction to morality   1

chapter 2
The bases of morality and systems of belief   19

chapter 3
Religion   27

chapter 4
Some major religions   37

chapter 5
The place of religious and moral education   45

chapter 6
Culture and its meanings   52

chapter 7
The role of the artist in society   80

chapter 8

Artists and interaction with their audiences: public participation
in the arts and the value of art education   95

chapter 9

Art and music – artistic movements and the appreciation of
different styles of music   109

chapter 10

The media   125

index   145

dedication

I am grateful to Jeanette and Vanessa for volunteering to stand in front of Chiswick House to give some impression of its size while I photographed it. To Vanessa again for allowing me to print her article on Performing. To Stella for some useful BMJ material and for helping with the checking of the manuscript following the collapse of the Spellcheck facility. To Brendan for some interesting ideas – some of which I dared not use – and to Malcolm for his genial interest, especially in reference to Buddhism.

Without their help this book would still have been written. But the Barnes family would not have got their names on this page!   *JB*

I should also like to thank Aileen and her Ravenshead library staff for their patient and friendly help.

acknowledgements

The authors and publishers are grateful to the following for permission to reproduce material:

- Arts Council of England for the tables on pages 96 and 100, from Skelton, A. *et al* (2000) *Arts in England: Attendance, Participation, and Attitudes in 2001*, London, pp.23, 36–37.

- Bill Bryson for the extract on p.62, from *Notes from a Small Island*, Black Swan, a division of Transworld Publishers.

- BMJ Publishing Group for the extract on p.12, from Dyer, C. (2002) 'Dying woman loses her battle for assisted suicide', *BMJ*, 324, p.1055.

- Times Newspapers Limited, 2002, for the extract on p.35.

Every effort has been made to contact copyright holders and we apologize if any have been overlooked. Should copyright have been unwittingly infringed in this book, the owners should contact the publishers, who will make corrections at reprint.

Photo credits:

- Advertising Archives (p.69)
- Art Directors & Trip Photolibrary (p.43, top; p.55)
- Bridgeman Art Library (p.63; p.85, bottom; p.104; p.113, bottom)
- Bridgeman Art Library/Museum of Modern Art Paris (p.113, top right)
- Bridgeman Art Library/Saatchi Collection (p.112)
- Corel 44 (NT) (p.113, middle right)
- Corel 473 (NT) (p.113, top left)
- Corel 481 (NT) (p.113, middle left)
- Michael Holford (p.43, bottom; p.85, top)
- Sonia Halliday Photographs (p.41)
- Sonia Halliday Photographs/Bryan Cox (p.37)

Colour section:

- The Parthenon, Athens, Corel 84 (NT)
- The Wilton Diptych, National Gallery Picture Library
- The Mona Lisa, Corel 301 (NT)
- The Sistine Chapel (detail, The Creation of Adam), Corel 301 (NT)
- Mater Dolorosa, Scala Archives
- Woman Taken in Adultery, Bridgeman Art Library/National Gallery
- The Kitchen Maid, Corel 475 (NT)
- The Taj Mahal, Digital Stock 6 (NT)
- The Fighting Téméraire, Corel 137 (NT)
- Place du Théâtre Français, Corel 478 (NT)
- Le Moulin de la Galette, Corel 302 (NT)
- Bedroom at Arles, Corel 478 (NT)
- Broadway Boogie Woogie, Scala Archives
- Profile of Time, Bridgeman Art Library/Museum of Modern Art New York
- Cans of Campbell's Soup, Bridgeman Art Library
- Sydney Opera House, Corel 13 (NT)

introduction

The practical purpose of this book is to help you to pass the AS general studies examination with flying colours and to give you a good foundation for the A2 examination. In addition to this aim is a wish to help you to think about questions that are important to you and to society. Beliefs, values, moral reasoning and an understanding of the distinction between knowledge and belief are essential if you are to know where you stand on critical issues and if you are to be able to make important decisions. Naturally, this book does not teach you *what* to think but, through the issues that it presents, it tries to provoke thought and, in a variety of ways, it shows you *how* to think.

A study of the complex subject of culture helps us to understand the underlying beliefs and customs of our nation, religion and ethnic group – and the subgroups to which we belong. Many things that we take for granted are part of our culture. Collectively we condemn murder, brutality and theft and uphold justice and fair play. Knowing what makes up our culture gives us a sense of being part of society, but it can also be a starting point for changes in our beliefs and in our ways of doing things.

A knowledge of other religions can, at the very least, lead to a better understanding of people of different religious beliefs, so an account of five major religions is given in Chapter 4. Perhaps you will also become interested in other religions that, unfortunately, could not be included in this book.

An appreciation of the arts and a broad understanding of their historical development can be a great asset, extending one's interest in all aspects of life, refining one's senses and challenging the intellect. You may be surprised to discover that you already appreciate some of various forms of the arts. You may have actually participated in some of them. They are not all 'highbrow'. Find out more in Chapter 8.

The media are always with us. There are people who seem to believe everything they read in the newspapers and hear on radio or see on television. Sometimes it is easier to accept rather than question – but that kind of attitude means that we do not know the truth about events and situations reported. It is important to consider whether a story accurately reports something that really happened or whether it has been created to serve the newspaper more than its readers. When an election comes, many of our newspapers will be canvassing for their particular political party just as hard as the politicians and they will be feeding us their opinions as news. If we are not careful governments will be elected on slogans instead of on policies. It has probably already happened.

Censorship always means that something is being hidden from the public. Do we want this? Yes, if it truly is in the national interest, but what if the hidden part is obscene, likely to deprave or sacrilegious? There are those who would welcome such material and who would claim their rights as adults to have it available, but what if it is thought likely to corrupt children? It cannot be proved that moral behaviour has deteriorated because of the increasing freedom from censorship over the last 40 years.

These are all issues for you to think about. This is what we hope this book will do – give you controversial issues to think about.

The book contains some knowledge, some truth and, you may suspect, some personal belief. But you will not find much personal belief because the purpose of this book is to examine beliefs. We are not in the business of trying to influence you in any direction.

We want you to study the book, think about some of the questions raised, come to some conclusions and – of great practical importance – do well in your examinations. If anything is going to help you, this book will.

1

An introduction to morality

This chapter about morality and belief starts with an examination of knowledge, truth and belief and raises the question of how we face moral problems. This is followed by some moral dilemmas – situations involving a choice between two alternatives, both of which are problematic and likely to cause anxiety.

The chapter looks at the different ways in which a dilemma may be approached, showing that there is always a reason for our conduct, although sometimes the motivation is not easy to understand. Morality, in simple terms, is about knowing the difference between right and wrong. Making moral decisions is often hard because one's personal decision often affects other people.

Following sections on the definition of morality, on codes of behaviour, values and human rights, we examine the case of a terminally ill woman who sought the right for her husband to assist her in her own suicide.

After the final section on the law and moral codes you will find some notes on extended writing and essay writing and on small group discussion. It will be helpful to read these notes before starting any of the activities.

■ Knowledge, truth and belief

Perhaps some of you have led your lives being very practical and taking these three terms, 'knowledge', 'truth' and 'belief', for granted, so it may surprise you to know that people whom we call philosophers (thinkers) have been studying these concepts and arguing about them for centuries.

Take the example of a friend – let's call him Billy – telling you that another friend is not at home because, according to his mother, he is taking the dog for a walk. Suppose you accept that information. Is it knowledge? Is it true knowledge? You cannot be certain of the truth of the information because Charlie may have lied to his mother or his mother may have lied to Billy, or Billy may be lying to you.

While walking you come across Charlie with his dog. Your original unproved information is confirmed – it is proved true. If, on the other hand, you see Charlie with his girlfriend in a McDonald's your original information is shown to be false. The only true, reliable knowledge is that Billy told you that Charlie was out walking the dog.

When we take a break from our busy daily lives to start examining such questions and to seek answers we come to realize that knowledge can be arrived at in at least two ways:

- *empirically* – empiricism involves obtaining knowledge of the world through any of our senses (actually seeing Charlie walking the dog provides knowledge empirically);

- *rationally* – rationalism says that all knowledge starts with the mind. The mind works on and interprets all experience.

Both seem to have their limitations. Empiricism depends upon your senses working perfectly and there being no impediments to them. The person that you thought was Charlie *could* just have been someone who looked like Charlie. Rationalism is another essential means of gaining knowledge, but it could not have helped to establish the truth concerning Charlie's whereabouts.

We may discover new knowledge or work out new truths for ourselves by observation or by rational thought, although much of our knowledge and understanding is 'second-hand', learned from other people or from sources such as books, radio and television and the internet.

The traditional method that science has used to discover something new is called *induction.* This involves working from particular cases to the formation of hypotheses (generalizations). It involves seeing something happening regularly and believing that it is happening according to some rule or principle. It leads to *generalizations* based upon repeated occurrences of phenomena. The hypothesis (generalization) formed is there to be tested and possibly proved. In time, after what is considered to be a sufficient number of observations or trials, the hypothesis is accepted as 'new knowledge'. Much of our learning is by induction.

The question remaining is: how many trials and tests are needed to confirm a hypothesis? We never know whether somewhere there is an exception to the rule that has not yet observed. Karl Popper, an Austrian philosopher who taught logic and the scientific method at the London School of Economics, argued that the fault in the scientific method is that no matter how many times a phenomenon occurs the hypothesis is still provisional and is open to be disproved. His classic example says that however many white swans are observed it does not prove that there are no swans somewhere of some other colour, which have not yet been seen. Popper placed the emphasis on trying to disprove hypotheses rather than looking for cases that support them – a method that he thought can be self-fulfilling.

Rationalism starts with the mind, though empiricists may say that there is no evidence of the mind. There is a brain, which can be seen, but we won't go into that. Rationalism involves thinking things out to gain new knowledge. One well-established method is by a thinking device called a *syllogism*. It begins with two statements called premiss and ends with a 'must be' conclusion. Here's one:

1   In the human species only the female can become pregnant (main premiss).

2   This human being is pregnant (secondary premiss).

3   Therefore this human being is female (conclusion).

From two established truths a conclusion is reached. That conclusion is not reached by observation but it does depend upon knowledge learned (main premiss) and observation (secondary premiss). In syllogistic thinking, providing the main and secondary premisses hold good, then the conclusion is true.

analyse this

Work out a syllogism by yourself. Discuss your syllogism with a fellow student, asking for his or her critical examination and especially whether it holds good or not.

Belief

When religious believers talk about the one true god it is not a matter of observation or logical reasoning. It is more important than that, according to some people. Chapter 3 of this book discusses the question of belief and faith. They are both different kinds of knowledge; knowledge about matters unworldly. There may be no proof, but in basic questions such as the existence of God there is no disproof either. Belief and faith are very important to millions of people the world over, influencing and guiding the way they lead their lives and especially their relationships.

On the whole, mathematics provides truth without too much trouble – if you are good at maths, that is. What helped in the first place was the establishment of a numbering system. It is true that $3 + 7 = 10$, and it always will be true unless we start mucking about with the numbers. Take three apples. Put another seven apples with them. There are now 10 apples because that number of apples is exactly what we have learned to call '10'.

Language is vital in the establishment of truth. Not only in syllogisms but in everyday life language needs to be clear and adequate if we want our attempts at communication to be received as we intended. When we talk to or write to other people, unless we are relaying what somebody else has told us, what we are communicating comes from our life experiences, especially our relationships, and our thinking about our life experiences. The problem is that, in trying to communicate, we may be insufficiently precise, or the person with whom we are communicating may pick up implications not intended by the speaker. Here is an example of what is meant:

talking point

First speaker	As I was coming from the station last night I saw you going in the pub again.
Second speaker	So you think I'm always going boozing, then?

Remember that knowledge may be obtained from your own experience or your own thoughts. It is primary or first-hand knowledge, even if someone else has already obtained that knowledge. But most of our knowledge is secondary, obtained from outside sources such as television and books. You were not present at the Battle of Trafalgar in 1805, but you know that Nelson was fatally shot on board his ship, HMS *Victory*.

Is morality a question of faith in religious commandments or is it based upon non-religious, logical conclusions? Why should we be honest instead of dishonest? In considering moral questions the outcome is likely to be different according to whether one has:

- knowledge and understanding;

- a regard for truth and honesty;

- a basis of belief, either religious or secular.

Nevertheless, two people sharing the same belief and the same views and outlook may come to different decisions when facing the same moral problem. A moral code does not come with a set of instructions. You have to work at it.

■ Moral dilemmas – a few examples

> I think your hat is lovely.

What do you think about the following incident? Emily's aunt, who is very proud of her new hat and finds it very elegant and stylish, asks Emily's opinion about it:

talking point

Aunt	Do you like my new hat, Emily? What do you think? It cost a fortune at Harrods!
Emily	No, auntie. It is the most abominable hat I have ever seen. Don't wear it when you go out, will you?

It was not a moral dilemma for Emily. She knew just what to say in reply to her aunt. She stuck to her moral principle that lying is wrong. So, was she right?

Moral dilemmas crop up all the time, sometimes over very serious or distressing issues where it is very hard to make a decision.

analyse this

Think about each of the following situations and try to come to a decision. What would your fellow students do?

- You have strong religious beliefs and at a party someone starts making religious jokes that offend you. Will you, for the sake of the party and your friends' feelings, say nothing, or will you protest?

- At a club you see a friend taking drugs. Will you ignore it or report the matter to the management, to his or her parents, or to the police?

- A few days before your general studies examination your friend offers you a copy of the actual examination paper. Will you accept it or reject the offer?

■ Moral principles – and the difficulty of always abiding by them

A person's morals may spring from religious beliefs or from a view of the world and society. In other words, they may be based on religious or secular grounds. It may seem that religious beliefs are more influential, but it depends upon the strength of religious commitment in relation to personal and social need. Consider the following examples. They are quite common occurrences.

- A Catholic, forbidden by the Pope to use artificial methods of birth control or to have an abortion, may, because of personal and family pressures, resort to either or both of these modern facilities. Catholicism does, of course, offer confession of sin, repentance and forgiveness.

- Take the case of a parent, religious or non-religious, who is opposed to private education on the principle of equality of education for all. If that parent can afford private education and the local school has a poor reputation for discipline and academic results, should he stick to his principles and send his son to that downbeat local school or, thinking that private education will be better and more pleasant for his son, pay for him to go the private school?

- Another parent, religious or non-religious, opposed to private healthcare on the grounds of equality of healthcare for all, sees a daughter suffering in pain. There is a long waiting list for treatment. Should that parent go against the equality principle and pay for private treatment for the daughter or should he let her suffer for his principles?

analyse
this

a question of conscience

On examining your bank account you discover that your bank has wrongly credited your account with £1000. Is this your lucky day? What will you do?

If you decide to keep quiet and keep the money will you do so without any feelings of guilt or attacks of conscience whatsoever? Or will you try to make your decision seem reasonable, acceptable or even sensible? You might try to justify it by any of the following ideas:

- It is not your mistake so why should you bother to tell the bank?

- No individual is going to suffer – only the bank, and the bank has got plenty of money.

- It is just you and the bank, no social harm will be done.

- You need the money, probably more than most. The bank won't miss it.

- It is not theft. You didn't steal it. It's a bit of luck.

Is it a real temptation, even for those who are generally honest? Discuss the problem with a small group of fellow students.

Questions

1 What would you and they do?

2 Is it dishonest to try to keep the money?

3 Five reasons have been given for trying to keep the money. Try to think of the same number of reasons for informing the bank of its mistake.

4 Are all your reasons personal, or are any of them social reasons – 'for the good of society'?

5 If you personally would decide to tell the bank, would it be a matter of conscience or would it be for some practical reason, like fear of being found out?

If you discovered that the bank had wrongly credited your account and you just left the money there, you would not be breaking the law but you might be going against your own moral code. If you started spending the money you would be breaking the law. *People go to jail for it!* Note that you can act immorally without breaking the law.

Overheard on a bus

First passenger	Would you ever steal?
Second passenger	It all depends. I wouldn't steal from my family or friends, probably not from any person, but from a factory or other place of work, that's different. I mean, if I took a packet of drawing pins and some sticky tape from the office just to decorate our sitting-room for Christmas, where's the harm? The firm's got plenty. Other people do that sort of thing.

The second passenger could have answered the question in one word, which is . . .?

analyse this

Every so often throughout this series you are given an opportunity to do an independent presentation for your group. Make a presentation on the theme 'honesty and truthfulness are always the best policy'. Cover it from all aspects, including the personal and social angles, and the law. Look in the newspapers or watch television for examples to support your presentation, or even look to your own personal experience.

You could also deal with the 'it all depends' factor or use the example given previously of Emily and her aunt's new hat as an illustration.

■ What does the term 'morality' mean to you?

Try to define 'morality' and jot down what you think a code of moral behaviour should include. Will your list include some things that you ought to do as well as things you ought to avoid?

Where did your ideas come from?

- Your religion?
- Your general ideas of what is right and wrong, what is good and bad?

All religions have something to say about behaviour but there are people who have been brought up without any religion and have no religious belief. What about them? This is a question to be examined later on in this book, but you should think about it now.

■ Morality – a definition

Morality is a standard of human behaviour based upon what is generally and commonly agreed to be right or wrong. For the believer in God, morality is the standard of behaviour that God demands of human beings. It may be impossible to achieve, but some may come much closer to it than others. For non-believers it may be a code that they think is necessary if human beings are to be able to live together in a reasonable state of harmony and safety.

■ Values and codes of behaviour

Our codes of behaviour have developed from what have become socially agreed and accepted values:

- Some values are eternal.

- Others are comparatively recent.

- Some of our values spring from the old religious laws.

- Others have developed as the world has become more democratic and more concerned with the life of the individual.

- New values have to be worked out as science presents the world with more social dilemmas. In 2002 there were some frozen fertilized human egg cells. The mother of these cells wanted to have a baby from them. The father, who was separated from the mother, refused to give permission, so the mother sought a change in the law. This is a very sensitive legal and moral question.

- Some values are basic to the continuation of life in society. Others are less so, but they can be important in relationships between people and in the running of organizations.

Here are some values. Look at them very carefully. Which ones are really important?

- sanctity or inviolability of life
- justice
- liberty
- religious values
- equality
- peace
- love
- mercy
- concern for others
- charity
- democracy
- honesty
- work ethic and duty
- tolerance
- multiculturalism.

Add any that you think should be included.

Values vary between and within societies

Values may be different between different countries and may also differ between groups within the same country.

A good example of this is capital punishment. This country has abolished capital punishment. Other countries still carry out the punishment and in the USA some states have abolished capital punishment whereas others maintain it.

In 2002 northern Nigeria, which applied *shariah* law, condemned a woman found guilty of adultery to death by stoning. The southern part of the country and the central government are opposed to such practice.

key term

shariah

Islamic law.

Within the Anglican Church (Church of England) there are some parishes (areas with their own church) that welcome women priests and other parishes that refuse to consider them.

analyse
this

Study each of the following statements and decide which particular value – or values – apply:

1   Everyone should be allowed to die naturally.

2   In some countries people can be imprisoned for years without being charged or tried for any crime

3   Wealthy countries like Britain, Germany, France and the USA should do more to help poor countries.

4   I've not seen my elderly neighbour come out for a week. I'll just pop round to see if he's all right.

5   All applications for this job are welcome, regardless of sex, race, ethnic background, religion, age or any disability.

6   A teenager sitting in a bus offers his seat to an elderly person who is standing.

7   The elderly person says, 'No thank you. I can manage.'

8   I cannot stand his religious or his political views, but he is just as entitled to them as I am to mine.

■ The United Nations Declaration of Human Rights

In 1948, despite the religious, political, economic, historical and cultural differences between nations, the United Nations agreed the Universal Declaration of Human Rights. It represents a code of behaviour for all countries. This Universal Declaration included the rights to:

- life
- liberty
- education
- equality before the law
- freedom of movement
- freedom of religion
- freedom of association
- freedom of information
- a nationality.

This UN declaration represents a moral code for the nations of the world.

analyse this

motor neurone disease

Motor neurone disease is an incurable progressive type of paralysis. Among its symptoms are cramp and a quivering of muscle fibres. It affects most parts of the body including speech and breathing.

***'Dying woman loses her battle for assisted suicide'*, Clare Dyer, legal correspondent, BMJ**

A terminally ill British woman with motor neurone disease this week lost the final round of her legal battle for the right to have her husband help her to commit suicide without risking prosecution.

The European Court of Human Rights ruled that Diane Pretty's rights were not violated by the ban on assisted suicide in the United Kingdom or by the director of public prosecution's refusal to give an assurance that her husband, Brian, would not face criminal charges if he helped his wife to die.

The Strasbourg court was the last hope for Mrs Pretty, after first the High Court and then the House of Lords turned down her plea. The 43 year old mother of two, whose case was expedited because she has only months to live, wanted to avoid the 'distressing and undignified' final stages of motor neurone disease.

But the seven Strasbourg judges ruled unanimously that articles 2, 3, and 8 of the European Convention on Human Rights – the rights to life, freedom from inhuman or degrading treatment, and respect for private and family life – were not breached in her case. The court held that the state was not under an obligation to sanction steps to terminate a life to avoid the inhuman and degrading effects of an illness.

Suicide is not a crime in the United Kingdom, but assisting another to commit suicide is a serious offence. The judges said that 'To seek to build into the law an exemption for those judged to be incapable of committing suicide would seriously undermine the protection of life – which the 1961 Suicide Act was intended to safeguard – and greatly increase the risk of abuse.'

After the judgement, Mrs Pretty, who can say only a few words with the help of a voice synthesiser, said: 'The law has taken all my rights away.'

Dr Michael Wilks, the chairman of the BMA's ethics committee, said: 'In spring 2000 the BMA held a two day conference to promote the development of consensus on euthanasia and physician assisted suicide. Overwhelmingly, BMA members . . . agreed that they could not recommend a change in the law to allow euthanasia and physician assisted suicide.'

(Source: www.bmj.com/cgi/content/full/324/7338/629?maxtosh.../
2002&resourcetype=1.2.3.4.1.)

key terms

suicide

Purposely killing one-self. It is not a crime in this country.

assisted suicide

This happens when someone helps another person to commit suicide. Assisting in a suicide is a criminal offence.

euthanasia

Mercy killing. Causing the gentle and painless death of someone who is incurably ill and suffering. Generally the doctor will administer a drug. It is not allowed in this country, although it is in Holland.

Consider the case of suicide assisted by a loved one or by a doctor. Some of the most common arguments for and against assisted suicide appear as the following statements.

For:
We have a right to have our suffering ended and if we cannot do it ourselves we must have help from someone.

Against:
The end of suffering does not justify the killing of one person by another. Life and death are God's decisions.

For:
It can be perfectly controlled if it is assisted by doctors.

Against:
Doctors do not always make the correct medical and moral decisions.

For:
A loving wife or husband is the best one to assist in a suicide.

Against:
Can you be sure of a wife's or husband's love and that they will assist in the suicide purely out of love and not for selfish reasons?

analyse this

Discuss the question of assisted suicide and then write about 300 words on this controversial subject. It should be in essay form. (See notes at the end of this chapter on writing essays.)

- You may develop any of the ideas above, but you must develop your own ideas as well.

- You should think about the moral and practical issues and the related religious issues – where you think it appropriate.

- Your clear and clearly expressed thoughts on this controversial topic are very important, and whatever your views you need to present a reasoned and balanced account.

analyse
this

is the law of the land a moral code?

No. It is a civil code that tries to ensure that people live together sensibly and safely with rights and responsibilities. The law of the land may seem to be a moral framework to some people because it includes ancient religious laws such as those against murder, theft, lying and cheating. But the law changes, is added to as society develops technologically, socially and politically. Soon after the first car was made in the late 1880s we had to make laws about driving, road usage, licences, driving tests, vehicle testing and drink driving, mainly for reasons of safety. These were not specifically matters of conscience, but matters of common sense.

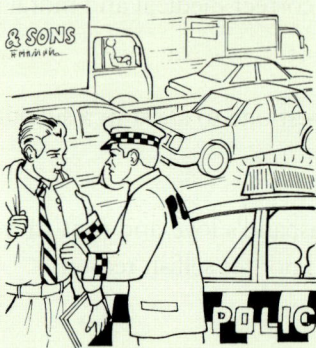

In this country, physical homosexual relations between consenting adults have not been against the law since the late 1960s. However, in 1895 Oscar Wilde, the famous playwright, was imprisoned for homosexual offences. Is this a moral question? Some people, some religions, some ethnic groups and some countries still think so. Morality was the basis of the old law; individual freedom and equality were the reasons behind its abolition.

Most people accept the law as sensible, on the whole, for the sake of the preservation of society, and others conform to it because they do not wish to be punished.

The law does not set out to shape people's moral codes. In many cases of immoral conduct the law is not interested.

Different people have different levels of morality. What sometimes makes life complicated is that people's standards vary according to particular situations. Is it wrong to steal? You will probably agree that it is. But is it always wrong in every case? During the early part of the nineteenth century the poor were likely to be transported to Australia chained in convict ships for as little as stealing a loaf of bread when hungry. Were they sinners? Morality is not straightforward, is it?

Questions

1   Which of the following is true according to the paragraphs above?

a   The purpose of the law is to maintain the moral standards of the people.

b   The law exists to bring old religious laws up to date.

14

c   The law is there to control people's behaviour.

d   The law exists to try to help people enjoy their rights and to live their lives responsibly and safely.

2 The law changes:

a   because of technical developments;

b   because of changes in the public's moral attitudes;

c   because ancient laws become out of date;

d   because of the reasons given in a and b.

3 Which of these statements is true?

a   The law is never concerned with matters of morality.

b   There are questions of morality that are covered by the law.

c   According to the paragraphs above, the law's purpose is to preserve society.

d   You will never be punished for swearing at a traffic warden.

4 Morality is not straightforward because:

a   society does not change, but morals do;

b   people fail to keep to their standards of morality;

c   some people have very low standards of morality;

d   people's standards of morality differ and judgements often have to be made according to the particular situation.

5 Which of the following statements best describes the main theme of the passage?

a   Society needs morals and laws.

b   The law has to adapt to change and individuals sometimes have to adapt their moral codes according to particular circumstances.

c   People either accept the law because they think it is right or because they wish to avoid being punished.

d   The law exists to protect the rights of the people.

Fixed code, flexible application

When it comes to a question of morality it is rather like having a metre stick in the cupboard at home and a tape measure in your pocket. The metre stick, made of wood, is always the same length. For everyday use, we employ the tape measure because it is easier to carry around and is more flexible, but it may stretch or shrink. We get by with it well enough. But if we want an exact measure we have to get the metre stick out of the cupboard.

A moral code is like the metre stick, something stable to refer to, but the way we deal with dilemmas in life, to get by, is rather like using the tape measure: convenient, adaptable, but not strictly accurate.

Consider some important aspects of moral codes: killing, stealing, lying. Are they:

- intrinsically wrong – wrong in themselves – because they are sins against God;

- wrong because they corrupt the performer of these actions;

- wrong because they hurt someone?

Social wrongs are acts that can upset other individuals as well as those affected and they are examples of the sort of behaviour that, if allowed to spread, will cause distrust in society and disturb its balance.

Why are some actions considered right and good and others not so? Religion tells men and women not to covet their neighbours' spouses. Why not, if the neighbour's wife or husband is more appealing than your own? It happens at all levels of society, right up to the royal family.

■ What do you think now?

You have almost reached the end of this introductory chapter and should have a good general idea about the nature of morality. Look back and reflect on what you have studied. Most of the questions you have had so far have been specific, about one aspect of morality. Now the chapter ends with questions that are more general, asking you to think about the nature or value of morality.

analyse
this

Here are some questions for thought. The first question is based on the passage 'Is the law of the land a moral code?' Questions 2 and 3 are extra, voluntary assignments for those who want to get their teeth into the whole question of morality. At the very end of this chapter you will see a section giving a few notes on writing essay-type answers.

Questions

1 Write about 250–300 words showing why the law has to be adaptable and why it cannot include all matters of morality.

2 Morals are matters of opinion. Discuss this statement

3 Without some generally accepted moral code, on top of the law, life would still be very unpleasant. Do you agree?

■ A few notes on extended writing or short essay-type answers

1 For this type of answer write in continuous English, using sentences and paragraphs.

2 Stick exactly to the question, underlining key words on the examination paper if it helps you to focus upon the detailed task.

3 If you are struggling for ideas, do a spider diagram.

4 From the brainstorming exercise pick out the key ideas and organize them into planned paragraphs.

5 Think of an introduction. The important thing is to see the skeleton of your answer before you start writing it. Begin thinking of your final paragraph, which may be a summary of the main ideas or, more intellectually, a conclusion. Introductions and conclusions are normally shorter than they are for a full essay.

6 Where you are arguing for a particular case remember to give your own views as well as to deal with the opposing case. Opinion, reason and balance are important.

7 Remember to give reasons where they are needed, as well as evidence and examples.

8 Have a look at the following advice too.

■ Advice on small group discussion

Obviously you will not be asked to enter into an oral discussion in the examination but, as in all examinations, you will be required to *think*, to *interpret*, to *reason*, to *give reasons* and *to weigh up evidence.* Trying to express your views in discussion and being prepared to encounter opposing views helps to bring your own opinions into focus, to sharpen or to modify them. You can become more precise, more definite, less tentative. Remember that the point of a discussion is to learn and not to win. You have to accept opposing views with some grace.

2

The bases of morality and systems of belief

This chapter considers the question of morality from a religious standpoint and from a secular (non-religious) standpoint. An examination of religion and an account of five major religions can be seen in Chapters 3 and 4, respectively. This chapter examines the durability of religion and its acceptance as a basis for the moral codes of believers. Although non-believers have no god they are nonetheless able to form and abide by a moral code, generally through a rationalist philosophy. Utilitarianism will be considered here as a means of making moral decisions, and this chapter will stress that believers and non-believers share many values. This is illustrated by a brief summary of two political philosophies and how they may or may not relate to religious beliefs.

■ Religion – its endurance and moral influence

Religion has lasted and influenced many people's lives for many centuries. Ray Billington, in his book *Living Philosophy* (1995), believes that religion has been important in the lives of the people in all civilizations. Often persecuted, religious believers have 'gone underground and survived in the face of opposition, defamation and execution.'

In the old Soviet Union the government was undemocratic, authoritarian and atheistic. Religion was persecuted and churches became museums but when, at the beginning of the 1990s, after 70 years, the regime gave way to democratic pressure and the people gained freedom, they flocked back to their places of worship.

Religion has endured and has provided a moral code for millions of people the world over. In the vast majority of religions this code comes from their belief in a god who has set down laws directing their behaviour. An example of such a code is the Ten Commandments (see Chapter 3). Under these commandments murder, theft, lying and adultery are sinful because they are acts against the will of God and God is the omniscient (all-knowing) Lord.

For the practising believer of any religion, regular prayer, devotion and attendance at the place of worship all reinforce the idea of God's existence, his omnipotence (all-powerfulness), his omniscience and, in particular, the idea that He knows what is good, what is right, what is best. From the commands of God, whether He be the God of the Old Testament Bible, or Allah of the religion of Islam, religious scholars and leaders have tried to decide the difference between moral and immoral actions and they have laid down comprehensive codes of behaviour.

Questions

Answer the following questions on the above passage. Write two or three paragraphs for each question.

1 Explain in your own words some of the difficulties religion has had to face.

2 The passage does not explain why religion has survived over the centuries. Try to think up some reasons for its survival.

3 Describe how religion has affected the lives of believers.

■ The atheist and the moral commandment of God

The idea of God's will as a basis for behaviour has been dominant throughout the centuries and, despite new approaches to life and morals in the seventeenth and eighteenth centuries, when philosophers began to develop a more secular approach to morality, God's will is still the basis for the code of morality and standard of behaviour for millions of people.

Most religions have a codified system of belief and behaviour. Religion itself, its scriptures, its precepts, its professionals (priest, iman, rabbi, guru) help to define morality for the believer and provide some basis for daily life and decision making.

The atheist, not believing in God, may very well excuse him or herself from any moral command attributed to God, arguing that there is no such thing as a god and therefore no such thing as God's will. However he or she may still live within the law, if only to avoid ending up in jail.

Atheism is probably considered by believers to be negative for it is a denial of God's existence and, by implication, His law. By itself non-belief will not provide any kind of stimulus for morality or for decision making, or for a way of life. However, and this applies whether we have religion or not, we have many sides to our lives, depending upon our personalities, nature and experiences, and they are all likely to influence our moral beliefs.

A Christian, Jew, Hindu or Muslim may be a stockbroker, a dress designer, a toilet attendant, a pop-star, an Oxfam worker, a Conservative, a supporter of the RSPCA, a member of Amnesty International or the National Trust and a believer in the power of reason. So may an atheist! Positive atheists believe in the power of reason and try to use it.

analyse
this

the atheist

We must all have met people raised in a non-religious environment, whose lives are just as morally acceptable as those of people raised in a religious context. Sometimes, in fact, the boot is on the other foot. The South African Nationalist leader, the atheist, Nelson Mandela was prepared to spend decades of his life in prison rather than modify his opposition to that country's apartheid policy. We thus have the example of an atheist sacrificing his freedom rather than compromising himself on the apartheid policy, viewed by many people outside South Africa as the most unjust and inhumane of governments since that of Nazi Germany; but those who defended it were starkly religious Afrikaners who believed, sincerely and devoutly, that apartheid was God's will.

(Source: Ray Billington, *Living Philosophy*.)

(Mandela was released from prison in 1990 at the age of 71, after serving 26 years for sabotage and treason. He became the first leader of a new multiracial South Africa.)

Questions

1 Write a paragraph to explain what 'apartheid' was.

2 Explain in a few sentences the main point of Billington's article on Mandela .

3 Mandela was not motivated by religion. He was an atheist. Nor was he motivated simply by his atheism. What do you think, in your own words, was the motivating force that gave him the strength to face a long imprisonment?

analyse this

'Atheists are just as likely as religious believers to accept suffering for their beliefs.' Study this statement. Do a 10-minute presentation to prove the statement, but do not use the case of Nelson Mandela. You will need at least two examples, a believer and an atheist, to illustrate your point. You need to explain exactly why each is prepared to suffer. Give your opinions and your reasons for them.

key terms

apartheid

Well, on this occasion, look it up yourself and write out the definition.

afrikaners

Afrikaans-speaking white person in South Africa, especially one of Dutch descent.

There are various secular bases for morality:

- a belief in the need to preserve society and to help it to promote security, health and happiness;

- a desire to conform to society's norms of behaviour and to be generally accepted;

- a well-developed conscience that leads one to want to help rather than hurt others;

- holding a particular philosophy that provides a basis for morality – for example *utilitarianism*, a topic that follows after this section;

- a rational approach to life that leads a person to think things out logically;

- a political belief about the way society should be organized.

Utilitarianism and two of its exponents

In contrast to the moral commandment of God as a basis for morality, from the middle of the eighteenth century there developed a utilitarian philosophical approach (utilitarian means useful, of most benefit or of most good).

Jeremy Bentham (1742–1832)

If you ever go to University College in London you will come across an amazing sight in one of the entrances – the actual preserved and clothed skeleton of Jeremy Bentham, the London moral, political and legal thinker. Bentham formulated the utilitarian philosophy according to which every action taken has to be judged by the results it produces. He was concerned with causes and effects and wanted to inject *reason* into moral decisions, which would lead to the greater good or happiness of the individual or the people. Here are Bentham's own words taken from his *Introduction to the Principles of Morals and Legislation*:

> *By the principle of utility is meant that principle which approves or disapproves of every action whatsoever according to the tendency it appears to have to augment or diminish the happiness of the party whose interest is in question.*

Think about it. An action is good or moral if the result is good, or is the best possible outcome. Bentham criticized any attempt to make moral decisions according to the individual's own intuition, according to her or his own subjective approval or disapproval, without considering the consequences. Such action he described as selfish and dictatorial.

John Stuart Mill (1806–73)

Mill was Bentham's godson, but he was buried normally; only his ideas are preserved. He became a disciple of Bentham. He emphasized that the utilitarian philosophy meant that the individual should not simply consider his own good, his own happiness in any decision, but the good and happiness of the greatest possible number of people. To Mill, happiness was not simply a life of lazy luxury, but a life of quality through the arts, humanities and sciences.

An interesting snippet from his life, which exemplifies his attitude, was that in his late teens he was arrested for giving out birth-control literature to the poor in London. Birth control in 1824! It was still considered scandalous more than 100 years later.

The slogan 'the greatest good for the greatest number' has developed from utilitarian philosophy.

Thinking about utilitarianism

Think about utilitarianism. Does it make sense? Is anyone likely to take an action that goes against her or his own interests for the sake of the greater good of society? Yes. It is sometimes called 'sacrifice'.

It's less trouble for the bank if I keep the money!

Utilitarianism is a pragmatic or practical approach, one that immediately suggests common sense, which is rather different from the law as dictated by God. Or is it always common sense?

Returning to Chapter 1 and the £1000 wrongly credited to your account, how can you solve the moral dilemma, either to keep the money or tell the bank? Obeying God's command not to keep the money is comparatively easy, for morally there is only once course of action you can take, since it is not your money – unless you are overcome by temptation. But what about the utilitarian approach?

Who is going to judge the likely results of the two alternatives and which will give the greater happiness? The only person in a position to decide is the one who has the money in the account. Will that person telephone the bank manager, keeping his or her identity a secret, to discuss which is the greater good, keeping the money or letting the bank get it back by revealing his or her identity. That would only happen in *Monty Python*!

Questions

1   Which of the following best fits in with the utilitarian approach?

   a   In moral decisions be guided by what is useful.

   b   In all decisions please yourself.

   c   Always take the most practical course of action.

   d   In general terms society should be guided in its decisions by what will satisfy the needs of the majority of the people.

2   Which of the following statements is/are true, according to Bentham's and Mill's philosophy?

   a   Intuition is the best guide in making moral decisions.

   b   Reason is more important than intuition in making moral decisions.

   c   Utilitarianism is selfish and dictatorial.

   d   Utilitarianism may mean ignoring your own needs for the greater good of society.

3   In about 200 words express your views on the utilitarian approach, describing any strengths and weaknesses that it has. You may wish to consider solving moral dilemmas by this approach.

Utilitarianism is more of a formula for making decisions – based on the idea of the greatest good for the greatest number – than a system of beliefs about what should be done. In contrast, we now look at two political beliefs, conservatism and socialism, which have clear philosophies about how society should be organised.

Conservatism

Classically and worldwide, conservatism embraces capitalism, an economic system in which the means of production, distribution and exchange (industry, commerce and finance) are owned and managed by private individuals or corporations. The system is one of private enterprise in which success or failure, profit or loss depends on the enterprise of, and the risk taken by, individual owners and business corporations. Competition is keen, but the system is thought to be better for the customer.

Socialism

Socialism argues that conservatism relies too much on the profit motive, which, it says, serves the owners of capital more than the general public. As a consequence socialism has traditionally advocated the public ownership of the means of production, distribution and exchange, and a more equitable share-out of the benefits. This is thought to be a better economic system and much fairer.

A conservative or a socialist may be utilitarian in approach. It may be impossible for a religious person to make moral decisions on the basis of utilitarianism. But if both conservatives and socialists believe that their political philosophies will lead to the greatest good for the greatest number then to that extent they are being utilitarian.

analyse this

This is based on what you have just read about conservatism and socialism but it is also related to religious belief. Consider these four people – A, B, C and D – and discuss the options in small groups. Remember the advice at the end of Chapter 1.

- A is a member of the Conservative Party and is devoutly religious.
- B is also a member of the Conservative Party and is an atheist utilitarian.
- C is a member of a socialist party and is a devout member of the same religious group as A.
- D is a member of a socialist party and is an atheist utilitarian, like B.

Would A and B have more in common because they are members of the same political party or would A and C have more in common because they are members of the same religious denomination? Discuss all the possibilities giving *opinions* and *reasons*.

analyse this

This chapter ends by giving you the opportunity to put together all that you have studied so far; to think about it and to apply it to different situations.

Look at all the questions below. They are concerned with utilitarianism and/or religion. Choose one of them to write about 300–350 words. It is important that in considering all the alternatives you express your opinions clearly and you state your reasons. (This may be a good time to look at notes for writing essay-type answers at the end of Chapter 1.)

Questions

1 The ship has sunk, most of the lifeboats have been destroyed. The two remaining lifeboats are overloaded and in danger of being swamped by the hoards of screaming people trying to scramble aboard them. A religious naval officer is in charge of one of the lifeboats – a sincere believer who upholds the sanctity of life. In charge of the other boat is an officer whose approach to life has always been utilitarianism. Describe the thoughts of the officers, the courses of action likely to be taken by each and the consequences of each action.

2 In July 2002 a painting by Rubens (1577–1640) entitled *Massacre of the Innocents* was auctioned at Sotheby's for £50 million. (According to the New Testament, King Herod (74–4 BC) ordered the massacre of new-born boys.) Referring to utilitarianism, explain why some paintings are worth a great deal of money when they bring happiness to only a minority of people. Justify or criticize the morality of this.

3 'Religious morality is like a metre stick, unchanging, reliable as a guide to behaviour, therefore it gives a more secure foundation to one's life and behaviour than any philosophy that requires people to consider the consequences of every action.' Express your views on this statement.

3

Religion

This chapter explains the origin of religion, why the ancients needed a religion, the essence of religion and how it differs from belief in a political/economic philosophy. It points out that there are differences in the degree of commitment of people to their religion and raises the question of whether religious belief affects people's lives. Working through this chapter you will find that it calls upon your own beliefs, whatever they are.

Paradoxically, it raises the question of tolerance by looking at intolerance but includes a significant paragraph on Buddhist moral precepts. Hopefully this chapter will prepare you for the following chapter, which looks at five major religions.

■ Concepts associated with religion

If the word 'religion' is mentioned what comes to your mind? Your own religion, if you have one, or any of the ideas in the following list?

- Bible
- Qur'an
- gods
- spirit
- soul
- beliefs
- faith
- prayer
- worship
- life and death
- salvation.

Defining religion precisely is not easy, but any definition will include some of these ideas, especially *god* and *faith*. All religions have some organized system of beliefs, but not all religions believe in god. Buddhism, for example, does not have a god, but it does believe in something super-natural – reincarnation.

Is belief the crucial element of religion?

Then what about communism, socialism, conservatism? They are all systems of belief, but they are not religions. They are political, social and economic systems of belief and the only real link with what we traditionally regard as religion is that they all contain an element of idealism, a conviction that some day these beliefs will be implemented and the world will be a better-run, happier place. Religion, in contrast, has faith in matters beyond reason and understanding.

What exactly is faith?

Faith is a special personal and religious experience, which can become collective in religious gatherings. Sometimes it is a feeling of quiet, confident belonging, protection and certain knowledge of the truth, supported by prayer and holy rites. Sometimes it can be a feeling of exuberance and bounding confidence and love. These different moods can be seen, respectively, in the quiet reflective prayer and solemn moments of worship in a church and the joyous outpouring of singing, clapping evangelizing religions.

According to the *Wordsworth Encyclopedia of World Religions*, in Christianity faith is: 'The divinely inspired response to God's historical revelation through Jesus Christ.'

Faith is stronger than belief. It is an absolute conviction, a confidence in, and a trust of something incomprehensible, such as God, His word, and life after death. Faith is not based on knowledge or reason. It leaves no room for doubt and can give great strength. The strength of faith enables believers to face persecution and even death for their beliefs. Hindu women, for example, have been known to throw themselves on the funeral pyre of their dead husbands as a religious act of purification for both of them.

'Faith' has a secondary meaning when it refers to one's religion, as in the *Muslim faith,* the *Hindu faith,* 'my faith', and so on.

Systems of belief

Religions are more-or-less organized systems of belief, prayer, devotion and ritual, which are concerned with the mystery of life, life's purpose, the supernatural, life after death and the inner self or soul. For the most part, believers attend places of worship, prayer and ritual: churches, mosques, synagogues, temples or other places considered spiritual or holy.

Religions and moral law

Most religions have moral codes or laws that, depending upon the particular religion, have been handed down by God or have evolved over the centuries or have been written out by scholars, taken from what they believe is the word of God.

A Jewish boy in the synagogue, reading from the law

analyse
this
the Ten Commandments

These are moral laws believed by Christians and Jews to have been given by God to Moses about 3300 years ago. You can read all about it in the Bible, Exodus 20, and in the succeeding chapters you find God's laws in greater detail.

The Ten Commandments are:

1 Do not worship any gods but me.

2 Do not make or worship idols.

3 Do not misuse my name.

4 Keep the Sabbath day holy.

5 Respect your parents.

6 Do not kill anyone.

7 Do not commit adultery.

8 Do not steal.

9 Do not be a false witness against anyone.

10 Do not have designs on anyone's wife, slaves or possessions.

There then follow laws dealing with murder and abuse, responsibility of owners, laws about repayment, and moral and religious laws. Punishments are laid down, too. Many of the laws are designed to promote social harmony and give guidance in dealing with disputes between people.

Some of the detail is interesting. For instance, if a burglar is caught in the act at night and is killed, the person who killed him is not guilty of murder. However, if the burglar is caught in the act and killed during the day the person who killed him is guilty of murder and the punishment for murder, as it states elsewhere in Exodus, is death (Exodus 22).

Questions

The following topics for investigation and thought are for mini-essays. Remember to look at the end of Chapter 1 for notes on extended writing. Do all three of them and take about 40 minutes for this.

1 List the commandments that are included in present-day law. Then discuss why they still exist and why the others do not appear in law.

2 These laws have been in existence for thousands of years. They are believed by Christians and Jews to have come from God. If you are not sure that they came from God, where do you think they came from? The first three laws are about God Himself.

3 According to Exodus 21, the punishment for hitting one's father or mother is death. This is not part of our law. Why do you think that it was once punishable and why is it not a part of our law today?

key terms

five pillars of Islam

See Chapter 4, the section on Islam.

reincarnation

The belief that when one dies the soul is transferred to another, new body.

■ The origin of religion

The earliest religions were attempts by people, without our modern knowledge of natural phenomena, to explain the mysteries of nature, of weather changes, of the sun's and moon's cycles and the mystery of birth and death. Survival was naturally their first priority, but human beings have always striven to understand their environment. Some early religions came to see the heavenly bodies as some kind of supernatural beings, like a god with influence over their lives.

An example of a fairly localized religion, whose origin is unknown, is Druidism, in existence over 2200 year ago. Since those times religion has become more sophisticated, more organized, more differentiated and more humane.

analyse this

ancient and modern religion

Julius Caesar came across Druidism when he invaded the Celtic lands of Britain and Gaul (France) just over 2000 years ago.

The religion was maintained and led by Druid priests, who, according to Roman historians, were also judges, philosophers, doctors and mystics, all rolled into one. It is recorded that the Druids believed in reincarnation, thought that the mistletoe plant was sacred, and held mystic rites in the sacred oak groves. Human sacrifice to the gods, especially of criminals, was also a feature of this religion.

Since those early times other organized, sophisticated religions have developed. The vast majority of people who nowadays adhere to any religion do not do so out of fear of the unknown or to please some god. They come to religion through the family, or through some kind of conversion after listening to a religious leader. What the most devout of them acquire is a firm belief, a faith and an understanding of the meaning and purpose of life, as revealed in the tenets of their religious faith.

There are different levels of commitment. Pious Christians go to church regularly, pray regularly and enter into the spirit of the religion. Sincere Muslims will pray five times a day and strive to uphold the five pillars of Islam. The faith of such fervent believers spills over into their daily lives and in their dealings with other people. However, in all faiths there are also those whose commitment is considerably less. They believe, but do not feel the need for such devotion and ritual or they are too busy in their daily lives.

Questions

Here are a few multiple-choice questions. Choose the best fit of the four options given in each of the following:

1 Which of the following statements is or are true?

   a Druid priests had many roles to play.

   b They thought that death was the end of life.

   c They were appointed by the Romans.

   d They did not see any need to make offerings to the gods.

2 Which of the following reasons explain why people are religious today?

   a They are frightened of death.

   b They are influenced by their background.

    c   They want to end up in heaven.

    d   They studied religious education at school.

3 Which of the following is the major change since the days of ancient Druidism?

    a   The belief in reincarnation has disappeared.

    b   Mistletoe has no significance now.

    c   Nowadays people have a greater understanding of the nature of religion.

    d   People are no longer killed in the name of religion.

4 Which of the following is the fundamental, the most important aspect of religion?

    a   faith;

    b   religious practice;

    c   helping others;

    d   worship.

analyse this

How does religious belief influence and affect people's lives?

Do a presentation for the rest of the class in which you try to answer that question. Your talk may be based on one particular religious faith or on religion generally.

It is controversial and your presentation should reflect that by dealing with the balance of evidence. Example, reason, proof and opinion are all needed.

■ Tolerance: what does it mean and how important is it?

talking point

a serious dialogue

Fred   Now, you take the French – they're arrogant.

Kevin	No, they're not. They tell lies. It's the *Russians* who are arrogant.
Fred	Russians? I thought they were warlike.
Kevin	That's the *Germans* for you.
Fred	But ain't the Germans know-alls?
Kevin	No, you're thinking of the *Italians* – the Eyeties.
Fred	I thought the Italians were lazy, lying around in the shade all day long drinking bottles of wine.
Kevin	Now you're talking about the *Spanish* – you know, dagos.
Fred	'Ere, they got some funny ideas about us, them continentals. Them Froggies think we're a load of cold-blooded, unfriendly wotsnames.
Kevin	What did I tell yer? Them French. They're jealous of us. All their women go around in black knickers, smelling of garlic and screaming, 'Oo la, la!'
Fred	I'd like to see that. Er, I mean, cor, it makes yer glad to be British. British Bulldog, eh! Fair-minded, tolerant, sportsmen.
Kevin	Mind you, the Scots are a bit mean and the Welsh are shifty. As for the Irish, they don't know nothing.
Fred	You said it. England for us! Specially the south. You can keep yer Lancashire 'ot pot, tripe and black puddin'. Give us jellied eels any day.
Kevin	London's the place. North London where the people are real mates you can trust, friendly, 'elpful. Trust 'em with yer life.
Fred	Up the 'Gunners'!
Kevin	What, Arsenal? That mob of ruffians. Boring old Arsenal!

Fred	Whadjer mean?
Kevin	Spurs is what I mean, mate. Tottenham 'Otspurs. Best football team in the world. Beat Arsenal anytime and they won't foul 'alf as much.
Fred	Listen, mate. You, you, you – I know where you live.

Questions

Read through the questions and the definition of toleration below. Then discuss in small groups the attitudes displayed in the above dialogue. (See the advice at the end of Chapter 1.)

1 Is this kind of conversation harmless?

2 Do you despise such people? Do you feel sorry for them? What is your reaction?

3 Do you think that racial intolerance and this kind of tribalism exists only among people like Kevin and Fred or do you think it occurs higher up the socio-economic scale. Evidence, especially from what you have picked up in the media, would be very useful.

Toleration means accepting and allowing differences between people in matters of race, religion, customs and opinions without attempting to discriminate or to deal differently, unequally or abusively with people who are different.

analyse this

toleration

Anyone for tennis?

A. *Pakistan has threatened to ban its Muslim tennis star from representing the country after he teamed up with an Israeli Jew for the doubles at Wimbledon. Last week the* Daily Mirror *told how Lahore-born Alsam-ul-haq Qureshi, 22, paired up with Israel's Amir Hadad, 24, and vowed to dedicate their success to world peace. Pakistan sport board director Brigadier Saulat Abbas yesterday said the government opposed the partnership and was considering turning its back on Qureshi. Sports board director Brigadier Saulat Abbas said: 'We officially condemn his playing with an Israeli and an explanation has been sought from him.' Since Pakistan has no links with Israel, Qureshi may face a ban. (Daily Mirror, 1 July 2002)*

I can't stand people who are intolerant!

B. *Buddhist moral precepts are based on the Dharma, and they reflect such eternal values as compassion, respect, self-restraint, honesty, and wisdom. These are values that are cherished by all civilizations, and their significance is universally recognized. Moral precepts that are based on such values or directed toward their realization will always be relevant to human society, no matter to what extent it has developed. (www.singnet.com.sg/alankhoo)*

C. *One quarter of the clergy in the Church of England are still opposed to women bishops, according to a survey published yesterday. Despite eight years passing since women priests were first ordained in England, 25 per cent of clergy and 17 per cent of laity believe that there 'should not be any women bishops anywhere.' . . . 20 per cent of clergy indicated that they might go so far as to leave the Church, with 5 per cent signalling a definite intention to leave . . .*

[One of the clergy said] 'Many clergy were confident in their own ministry as priests but "fearful for the future" if women were to be ordained bishops.' (The Times, 29 June 2002)

Question

When you have read the items A, B and C above write a brief balanced account about one of them in which you deal with the attitudes and beliefs expressed – about 150 words in length. You may prefer to argue both for and against these attitudes and beliefs.

Intolerance has always been with us. We come across it in our daily lives and on a larger scale it often leads to wars and suffering between different racial or religious groups. In 1478, the Spanish Inquisition was set up to investigate heresy (having a different belief from the one established) and it led to the torture and burning of suspected offenders. In the sixteenth

key terms

dharma

The true teaching.

laity

Member of the congregation, not the clergy. Non-professionals.

and seventeenth centuries in this country the growth of Protestantism resulted in bloodshed between Catholics and Protestants. And nearer to our present time we have the street battles between the Catholics and Protestants in Northern Ireland.

'The Holocaust' refers to one of the most shocking examples of cruel intolerance. Soon after Hitler came to power in 1933 he began his policy of discrimination against the Jewish people, later sending them to forced-labour camps and, under the 'final solution', he attempted to have them gassed in his notorious concentration camps. Millions of people were executed or gassed, not only Jews, but homosexuals, gypsies and the mentally retarded. Hitler blamed the Jews because they were not of pure German stock, and they became the scapegoat for all Germany's problems.

There is intolerance at all levels. There have been racial feuds in our cities and examples of racial discrimination in and by the police and the armed forces. Discrimination is closely allied with intolerance and is a way of punishing people who are different. Why is it that some people cannot stand differences?

At the micro level there can be intolerance between two people of different opinions, neither wanting to hear or understand the views of the other, simply wanting to defeat the other by thrusting his or her views down the other person's throat. Such intolerance gets no one anywhere.

Questions

1 Look at this proposition and then present two sides of the argument: for it and against it, and say what you think. Write about 120 words for each.

'When people are strongly believing members of a religious group, a political party or any group they should stick to explaining their beliefs and opinions and not condemn, criticize, mock or argue with other religions, parties or groups.'

2 What is the distinction between belief and faith?

3 Has religious morality had any effect upon our laws?

4 Does it matter that a large proportion of people in this country show no real signs of a religious belief?

5 The two biggest football clubs in Scotland are Celtic and Rangers. One is thought to be Catholic and the other Protestant. Which is which?

4

Some major religions

The Dome of the Rock, Jerusalem

This chapter begins with some statistics about religious beliefs, followed by a checklist that is useful for deciding whether any set of beliefs constitutes a religion and a table showing similarities and differences between the five religions. There is a brief description of these religions, none of which originated in this country but all of which are practised here. The first three: Judaism, Christianity and Islam all originated in the Middle East and they share many beliefs and practices. Some scholars consider Judaism to be the 'father' of the other two religions because it is the oldest.

The other two religions, namely Hinduism and Buddhism, originated on the Indian subcontinent and there are also similarities between them.

Throughout this chapter you should bring your own beliefs to bear upon what you read. As you study the different religions, whatever your own

key terms

OT and NT

Old and New Testaments.

Brahma

The supreme god and creator, inspiration for all the other gods.

The Trinity

Three in one: God the Father, God the Son, and God the Holy Ghost. Three revelations of the one God.

Pali Canon (or Tipitaka)

Words of the Buddha, the way to live to achieve enlightenment.

Vedas

Divine knowledge, hymns, prayers and ritual.

views, remember that millions of people are devoted followers of a religion and that their beliefs are very important to them, as are the beliefs of non-religious people.

■ Some statistics about religion

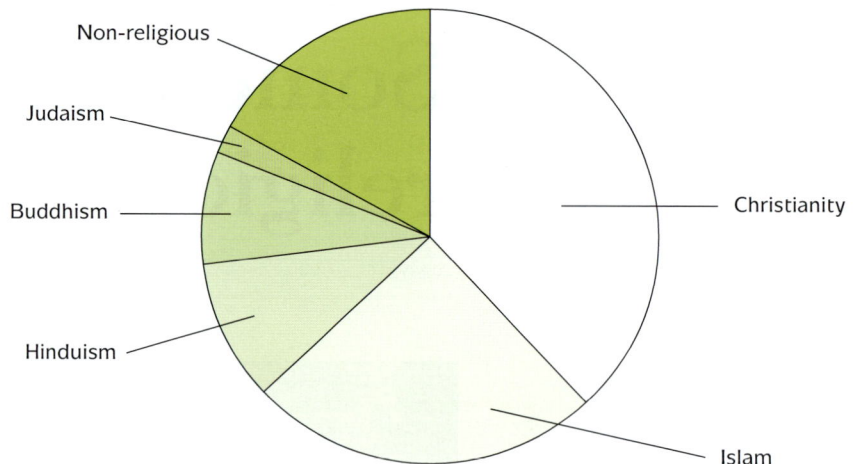

The pie chart shows the percentage of followers for the major religions. The figures for the five religions dealt with in this chapter plus the figure for non-religious groups are as follows:

Christianity: 2 billion   Buddhism: 360 million
Islam: 1.3 billion   Judaism: 14 million
Hinduism: 900 million   Non-religious: 850 million

(Source: www.Adherents.com.)

These numbers are estimates and cover the people who would identify themselves as adherents to the religion.

The numbers are not a league table. Many people would rather belong to a small breakaway group, regardless of its small congregation, than join with a larger group. Further statistics and details can be found at www.adherents.com/Religions.

analyse this

a checklist for religions

Before talking about the five religions it is useful to study the following checklist for religions. It is taken from W.P. Alston's *Philosophy of Language* and quoted in Ray Billington's *Living Philosophy*. Billington introduces the list by announcing it as one list of characteristics associated with the word 'religion'.

● Belief in supernatural beings (gods).

- A distinction between sacred and profane objects.
- Ritual acts focused around sacred objects.
- A moral code believed to be sanctioned by the gods.
- Characteristically religious feelings (awe, sense of mystery, sense of guilt, adoration, and so forth) which tend to be aroused in the presence of sacred objects, and which are associated with the gods.
- Prayer and other forms of communication with gods.
- A world view, that is a general picture of the world as a whole and of the place of the individual in it, including a specification of its overall significance.
- A more-or-less total organization of one's life based on the world view.
- A social organization bound together by the preceding characteristics.

Question

Is the list complete, or would you like to add to it or subtract anything?

■ A chronological line showing six major religions

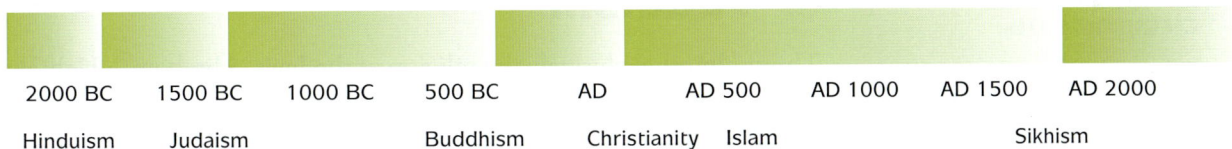

2000 BC	1500 BC	1000 BC	500 BC	AD	AD 500	AD 1000	AD 1500	AD 2000
Hinduism	Judaism		Buddhism	Christianity	Islam		Sikhism	

Note that Sikhism, an important religion from India, is included because it is a comparatively new religion. It contains elements of Hinduism and Islam, is monotheistic (believes in one god) and stresses equality, including equality of the sexes.

■ A comparative table for five major religions

Over the page is a quick-reference table to introduce you to comparative religion. Refer to this table as you read the brief accounts of different religions beneath it.

	Judaism	*Christianity*	*Islam*	*Hinduism*	*Buddhism*
Belief in a god	yes, one only	yes, Trinity	yes, Allah	many gods but Brahma is supreme	no
Belief in life after death	yes, most Jews believe	yes	yes	(see reincarnation)	(see reincarnation)
Belief in reincarnation	no	no	no	yes	yes
Scripture	Bible, O.T.	Bible, N.T.	Qur'an	Vedas	Pali Canon (or Tipitaka)
Belief in the soul	yes	yes	yes	yes	no
Place of worship	synagogue	church	mosque	temple	temple
Prayers and ritual acts	yes	yes	yes	yes	meditation (to achieve morality and wisdom)
Fixed beliefs and worship	yes	yes	yes	partly	no (emphasis on morality and non-violence)

(Different denominations and groups of the same religion will differ in some aspects of their fixed beliefs and practices)

Different denominations Variations or sects	(All these religions have them)
Moral values for life	(All religions – sanctioned by God, except for Buddhists, who have their own community ideas about the way of life)

key terms

circumcision
Cutting off, or cutting part of, the foreskin, a Jewish and Muslim religious rite.

Hebrew
Simply an ancient name for a Jew, also the language.

the Messiah
In Hebrew, the anointed one, or the liberator.

orthodox
Keeping strictly to traditional beliefs.

sabbath
A day of rest and religious observance.

Now that you have browsed through the table, does anything catch your eye or arouse your interest?

■ Judaism

This is almost exclusively the religion of the Jews. Abraham, a Hebrew prophet, made a pact with God about 3500 years ago, agreeing that his people would worship God as the one true God and that from thence all new-born male babies would be circumcized.

About 3300 years ago God gave his law to Moses on stone tablets, the most important part of the law being the Ten Commandments (see Chapter 3 of this book). Other instructions about living, including cleanliness and diet, were set out later. (See Leviticus in the Old Testament.) Pork was forbidden and all meat for consumption had to be free of blood.

Thus God's law was religious and moral and set out a social framework to encourage orderly community and family life. The Jewish Sabbath begins at sunset on Fridays.

The Old Testament promised the coming of the Messiah. For Christians, Christ is the promised Messiah, but the Jews, especially the Orthodox, still await His coming.

Question

Where do Jews worship? (See the table opposite.)

Window in Canterbury Cathedral showing the birth of Christ

■ Christianity

Christians believe in the one God of Judaism, the Creator of heaven and Earth, although it is not as simple as that. About 2000 years ago God sent his Son, Jesus Christ, a Jew, as the promised Messiah to live on earth and to bring a new message of salvation. It was Christ's destiny at the age of about 30 to be crucified to atone for the sins of the world and then to be resurrected to join God. For Christians, Christ is the way that they come to God the Father. See the New Testament, John 14: 'I am the way, the truth, and the life: no man cometh unto the Father, but by me.'

Although it is described as a monotheistic religion (believing in one god), the majority of Christians believe in the Trinity, one God in three persons, the Father, the Son and the Holy Spirit. One way of trying to understand this paradox is to think of it as God revealing Himself in three forms.

Much of the detail of the ancient law is covered under Christ's new order that to achieve salvation and dwell in heaven after death people have to accept Him as their saviour and to treat other people as they wish to be treated themselves.

key terms

atone
To make amends for sin, for example through repentance.

paradox
Two ideas that seem to contradict each other, though in fact do not do so.

resurrection
Being raised from the dead.

salvation
Deliverance from one's sin through atonement.

Question

Do you think that the principle of treating others as you would wish to be treated is a good basis for law?

key terms

shariah

Islamic law, religious and secular. Considered to be about the way God wants people to live.

■ Islam

Like Christianity and Judaism, Islam is a monotheistic religion. Members of this faith are Muslims and they worship Allah (God). This religion began when the prophet, Mohammad, received messages from the Angel Gabriel announcing the existence of the one true God. The angel spoke of the importance of repentance, the day of judgement and the resurrection in the next world where the believer would dwell in a high or low state depending upon the life led on earth.

The Qur'an is the holiest of Islamic books for it describes the word of God as revealed to Mohammad.

The Five Pillars of Islam form the foundation of the religion, urging Muslims to believe in Allah, pray, fast, give about 2.5 per cent of their income to the poor and make a pilgrimage to Mecca, where Mohammad, spent much of his life.

Muslims accept all the Old Testament prophets of Judaism and whereas Christians believe Christ to be divine, Muslims treat him as a prophet. Gabriel, the angel who revealed the word of Allah to Mohammad, is the same angel as the one thought by Christians to have told the Virgin Mary that she was to be the mother of Christ. Some of the laws of Islam are similar to the Commandments in the Old Testament. Muslims are expected to treat other people with consideration and to honour their parents. They also have dietary laws and Muslim boys are circumcized.

The most devout Muslims pray five times each day. Friday is their Sabbath.

Shariah is a comprehensive body of law derived from the Qur'an and the thoughts of the scholars and elders. It sets out rules for all aspects of life, not just the religious life and practice, but criminal law and family relationships. In some Muslim countries, notably Saudi Arabia, the law of the land is *shariah*.

Question

Who helped to start off both Christianity and Islam?

■ Hinduism

In this polytheistic religion (believing in many gods) there is no set creed (body of belief), nor does it have any prophets. Hindus believe in pantheism, that God exists everywhere in all things, so Hindus may worship anywhere.

The god, Brahma

It has no founder because it grew from a fusion of different beliefs up to about 4000 years ago. Hindu believers are mainly Indians or related people. Practice and belief vary according to sect and each family has its own particular god.

Reincarnation

When a Hindu dies his soul is thought to move on to another body. The state of one's existence in the new life depends on one's *karma* – deeds during the believer's present life.

Laws about the Hindu's duties are called *dharmas* and they deal with religion, law and order, and customs, in other words they are about the right way to live.

Hinduism has many gods and goddesses, but Brahma, Vishnu and Shiva are of prime importance. Brahma is the absolute, the supreme god. Gods have particular responsibilities, for example Shiva is the god of fertility and nature. Spiritual guides and teachers are called *gurus*.

To achieve the good life the Hindu has to try to attain four goals that deal with religious and secular duty, the pursuit of wealth and pleasure, and the highest state of all, *moksha*, which is a release from the burdens of one's actions and from the perpetual round of birth and rebirths. *Moksha* is thought to be a merging of the inner self with the absolute, Brahman. This state includes supreme knowledge and understanding and it involves devotion and duty at the highest level.

Question

What evidence is there to suggest that this religion is very different from the first three?

Gautama Buddha

■ Buddhism

Buddhism comes from the teaching of Gautama, a Hindu, born in India. Disillusioned with Hinduism and tired of his life of luxury, he abandoned his family for an ascetic journey in search of truth and the meaning of life. He received no divine revelation. He underwent a mental and spiritual struggle until one day, whilst sitting under a bo tree (a kind of fig tree), he reached the state of 'enlightenment' and thus became a *Buddha*, which means an enlightened one.

He described his experience to his followers, giving them his *dhamma*, or teaching, central to which is the belief that suffering, caused by desire, is the root cause of human misery.

The essence of Buddhism is the individual inner spirit or nature, which can be reached and discovered after a life of goodness and meditation.

key terms

ascetic

Religious person who is strictly self-disciplined, abstaining from all pleasurable temptations.

Belief and practice vary according to community and country, but there are two core beliefs:

- the Four Noble Truths explain that selfishness is the cause of suffering;

- the only escape is by following the Noble Eight-Fold Path, which encourages followers to lead a life of moral principle, compassion, non-violence, self-control, concentration and meditation, all leading to the perfect state of mind.

Following Hinduism, Buddhism believes in reincarnation. *Nirvana* is the highest aim. It is the state reached by Gautama under the bo tree. It is a state of inner freedom, of purity from greedy desire and hatred, and a detachment from worldly material affairs.

Question

How does Buddhism differ from all the other five religions?

analyse this

1 Study any two religions described. Compare them in about 300 words, commenting upon the similarities and differences. Use the comparative table as well. (Remember the advice at the end of Chapter 1.)

2 Do some research and prepare a presentation lasting about 10 minutes on one of the following topics. Illustrations may be very helpful – you could prepare them using a computer program such as Powerpoint. Remember that opinion, reason and interpretation are important, even if the topic seems to be mainly descriptive.

   a Any aspect of any of the religions in this chapter, such as beliefs, customs, ritual, places of worship and their significance.

   b Any religion not mentioned.

Questions

1 Which came first, Judaism or Christianity?

2 What are the meanings of monotheism, polytheism and pantheism?

3 Buddhism recognises no gods. What is it about the religion that is supernatural?

4 Give your own clear definition of tolerance.

5 What do you think is the purpose of religion?

6 Why do some people need it?

7 Why do others manage without it?

5

The place of religious and moral education

Religious and moral education? No, that's not my department. Er, whose is it then?

Who is responsible for religious and moral education? Somehow the vast majority of people develop a moral code as well as acquiring religious beliefs and faith. This chapter begins with faith schools and the responsibility of all state schools for religious and moral education. This is followed by discussions of educational aims and of the problem of making decisions on the basis of one's moral code. An important aspect of moral education is whether schools educate students into the prevailing culture by teaching conformity.

Finally the chapter examines some of the problems of moral education in a changing moral climate. In moral education, which is the better method of teaching moral education: a dogmatic approach or an approach involving the child? Who is the best person to give moral guidance: a religious leader, the parents, a health education worker or a teacher?

■ Faith schools

Nowadays most schools are secular although there are many religious schools. There are Church of England, Catholic, Muslim, Jewish schools and so on. Parents choose for their children to attend such schools, which promote their own beliefs and regularly hold services and ceremonies specific to that religion, including communion and mass in Catholic schools. The appropriate 'minister' of religion, priest or rabbi, will visit his or her school and exercise some influence upon it. One teacher exclaimed that the advantage of teaching in his Catholic school was that if they had difficult pupils they would 'just whistle for the priest!'

It is sometimes the case that faith schools have better academic and discipline records and perhaps this is because the parents have a faith and a moral code that they have tried to pass on to their children. It may also be because parents who choose a particular school on the grounds of better results and behaviour will make a point of supporting that school.

Where the faith school is better than the local secular schools then the pupils at the faith schools have better chances. Some educationists and parents oppose faith schools because they think such schools give students a better education and therefore a better start in life. What do you think?

All state schools, faith and secular, have a responsibility for religious and moral education.

analyse this

aims of education

The Education Reform Act of 1988 set out broad aims for schools:

- to promote the spiritual, moral, cultural, cognitive and physical development of all pupils; and

- to prepare pupils for the opportunities, responsibilities and experiences of adult life.

Compulsory religion

Both religious education (RE) and daily worship are compulsory unless parents request for their children to be excused. Most parents do not take up this right. The daily worship has to be mainly of a Christian nature, although if a majority of parents belong to other religions they may request a change in the nature of the daily act.

The aims of the national curriculum

The ways in which most schools deal with the spiritual and moral aims are broadly as follows:

- the teaching of religious education according to a set syllabus, generally by an RE specialist;

- daily assemblies;

- personal, social and health education;

- in other subjects, for example the study of a novel or a play in an English lesson can often generate ideas and discussion about morality and will often challenge one's moral code.

Religious education cannot promote spiritual development or provide religious experience, but it can help towards a greater understanding of, and a greater tolerance towards, those of different backgrounds and beliefs.

Question

Discuss and/or write about the following statement in about 350 words (the activity calls for reasoned argument for and against): 'Religion is a family or personal matter. Schools cannot provide any religious experience so any religious education should be left to the family. Religious education teaching and religious assemblies in all schools should be abolished.' (You choose whether or not to include faith schools.)

■ Moral codes

Most people come through into adulthood with some kind of moral code, either based upon a religious belief or upon some non-religious viewpoint. Codes are systems of beliefs that hang together, like the Highway Code or the Country Code. A moral principle, such as a belief in justice, should affect our behaviour and decision making in all our dealings with other people.

Moral codes and decisions

A code enables a person to make such statements as 'I will not do that because it is against my religious beliefs' or it is 'against my moral principles'. Jehovah's Witnesses (members of a religious movement) see Jehovah (God) as supreme, above all in this world, and from that belief they have strict rules about their dealings with any other authority. They will not permit blood transfusions, either for themselves or for their children.

Moral dilemmas

Chapter 1 has a section on the difficulty of making a decision when faced with a moral dilemma. You will realize from some of the examples that trying rigidly to abide by one's strict moral code can cause further moral anxiety. If a parent who is a Jehovah's Witness is told that his or her sick child's cure depends upon it having a blood transfusion then there is a real moral dilemma for that parent.

analyse this

education and conformity

Often, teaching morality has been seen as teaching people to conform. We conform to the law or we are punished. We conform to society's rules for behaviour or we are criticized and shunned. But society changes on all fronts, either dynamically or gradually, and not always for the best. George Bernard Shaw, an Irish philosopher and playwright, writing in

1944 in his *Everybody's Political What's What?* considered this question and presented a dilemma.

He argued that people have to behave in the way society expects them to behave otherwise they have to be shown the error of their ways and if they cannot change they have to be punished. But Shaw puts forward a dilemma. If everyone behaves in the same way how can there be any 'progress, change, evolution, invention, free will, free thought, free speech, personal rights and everything that distinguishes us from automatic stick-in-the-muds?' History shows many examples of people who have changed society by violating its laws. Women achieved the right to vote in 1928 after years of protest, demonstration and breaking the law.

Schools

Are students educated so that they can fit into society, or are students educated so that they can change society?

There is a great deal about schools that promotes conformity. The curriculum is imposed for most of a student's time in education and even in the Sixth Form, where more choice ought to be available, what one studies depends upon:

- one's previous examination results;

- which subjects can be taught by the school;

- whether a subject can be timetabled.

In addition to that:

- religious education and daily worship are obligatory, unless the parents decide otherwise;

- schools are places of rules and discipline codes;

- students have little say in the aims and the running of the school. If ever the management of a school makes decisions affecting the pupils, like shortening the lunch hour or introducing punishments, the students are seldom involved in these decisions;

- pupils have to be in set rooms at set times and for set lessons;

- in short, they are told what to do and when to do it and 'we'll let you know if we make any changes'.

If students do not grow up to learn conformity it is not because of a lack of practice. On the other hand, schools deal with large numbers and need to take measures to organize these numbers and promote orderly conduct so that learning can take place in a safe and proper environment.

The subjects that students study and, in general, the classroom experience aim to promote or at least provide opportunities for students to think for themselves and to make some choices.

Generally in lessons like personal, social and health education and in the humanities students are encouraged to express their own opinions, and art and drama look for individuality. Some schools and colleges do try to involve older pupils in some decision making.

Your ideas may be better than mine. And I hope they are!

If it is explicitly one of the school's aims to encourage independent thinking and the questioning of dogma (an authoritarian principle or rule) and where those aims are at least in part implemented then those schools will achieve some balance between the need to control and the need to encourage some healthy non-conformity.

But isn't moral education all about conforming? After the following activity you should read 'Moral education and changes in morality' below.

Questions

1 **Which of the following statements is true?**

a Society changes because we conform to society's laws.

b Society sometimes changes for the better.

c People obey the law because they do not want to be criticized or shunned.

d Teaching morality is really teaching people to obey.

2 **Which is true?**

a Shaw thought that people generally behaved how society expected them to behave.

b   He thought that punishment was a waste of time.

c   He believed that conformity could restrict progress.

d   He was opposed to free will.

3 The case study shows that:

a   Schools regularly involve students in decision making.

b   Schools can encourage either conformity or non-conformity.

c   Subjects and teaching can give students an opportunity to express their own views.

d   Generally it is better to accept things than to question them.

analyse
this

moral education and changes in morality

You were asked above if education was about conforming. It may be difficult to conform if morality changes.

Morality does change. Conduct once considered immoral may become more acceptable to society. Chapter 1 points out how values are affected by social change and particularly by scientific developments. The changing nature of morality is problematical, particularly for anyone concerned with spiritual and/or moral education.

Consider the following:

● contraception and birth control;

● abortion;

● sex outside marriage;

● living together as partners, instead of in marriage;

● partners choosing to have children;

● homosexual practice and gay rights.

This very list can cause an emotional reaction because some people oppose these practices on the grounds of religious or secular morality.

Two of them – abortion and homosexual practice – were once illegal. All of them were once considered to be immoral and they still have their opponents, but the social attitude towards these practices has gradually come to accept them since the 1960s. From some religious quarters there are strong objections. Catholicism and Buddhism both forbid abortion and Catholicism forbids all artificial means of contraception. There are also groups that are not especially religious that have strong views. The pro-life movement campaigns against abortion and post-sex contraception.

For anyone concerned with moral questions these are very sensitive issues. Who is the best person to deal with them:

- Parent?

- Priest or appropriate religious leader?

- Health education worker?

- Teacher?

How should they be addressed? The dogmatic approach says: 'This is what you should think and do and this is what you should not think and do.' The approach involving the child or student begins: 'Let's discuss the question. Some people think this, others disagree. What do you think?'

- A religious leader *may* have an easier task if he or she can refer to scripture to deal with this question, providing the 'learner' is a member of the faith.

- A religious parent may also refer to scripture and the moral code, though all parents will be concerned with the general and moral welfare of the child.

- A health education worker will probably deal with the practical issues and, for example, the advantages and disadvantages of each method of contraception, although the health worker may also have a moral code based on religious faith.

- A teacher will probably follow his personal, social and health education guidance notes, generally with some sensitivity and perhaps some anxiety. He or she may also have a moral code based on faith.

The personal example of parents, teachers and religious leaders is probably more influential than what they try to teach about morality.

Question

The following task is based on the general principles of this article on moral education and changes in morality, but it will be helpful to refer to the definition of morality given in Chapter 1. It begins: 'Morality is a standard of human behaviour based upon what is generally and commonly agreed to be right or wrong'. You may wish also to consider if there are any moral commandments which have lasted.

Consider the following proposition and then express your views in writing, in about 350 words, giving reasons and any evidence or illustration: 'Any definition of morality that refers to a standard of acceptable behaviour should include the words "at a particular time". Morality changes, conduct once condemned becomes acceptable. We have to change, too, and so does anyone involved in moral education.'

6

Culture and its meanings

This chapter begins with an induction exercise to help you start to think about the concept of *culture*. You will see some examples of the ways in which the word is used and then you will try to come to some conclusion about its meaning. It is how we learn most of our language. Think of all the words you know. You have learned most of them by experiencing how they are used, not by looking them all up in a dictionary!

This is followed by an introduction that gives some of the most important factors of a national culture and makes a passing reference to two sub-cultures, 'high' and 'popular' (or 'pop'). We are all generally aware that the cultures of other countries differ from ours in some ways and you are asked to compare the culture of two countries, using some given factors. Science has made life easier for us and given us greater freedom. It has changed the home environment and changed to some extent the way people live and communicate.

The case study, 'British culture and its subcultures', shows that with immigration and the presence of many people of different national and ethnic origins living in this country, some acculturation has taken place. In other words people have in some ways adapted to different cultures, and the town landscape, with its various places and institutions of different national and ethnic origins, has changed over the last 50 years. One of the points emphasized is that culture is dynamic; it changes.

Language is important in maintaining culture. It is important to acquire the major language of the country one is living in, not only to understand something of the main culture but to be able to cope with living in the country without depending on those who speak its language.

Without language, thinking is impossible and there is some evidence to show that different cultures may have different ways of thinking. Language and culture are mutually influential; each influences the other.

The article on sex and culture gives evidence of the changing nature of culture, whilst also pointing out that there are always subgroups at odds with mainstream culture.

There are case studies about cultural changes and cigarette advertising, and these are followed by a section on smoking and cultural change, which shows how attitudes and behaviour have altered since the link between smoking and cancer was made in the 1960s.

The case study that follows shows the differences in attitudes between Asian and Australian students, and the chapter concludes by showing some of the distinctions between high and pop culture.

analyse this

This is an induction exercise that will help you to grasp the meaning of the concept of 'culture'. The following four statements each use the word 'culture'. Study each example and then try to write your own definition of the word.

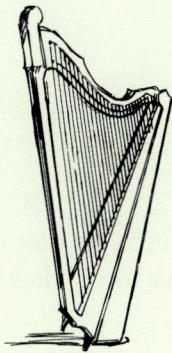

- 'A popular tradition of our culture, which distinguishes us from Europe – where they speak different languages from us – is our love of cricket. Another tradition, which distinguishes us from the USA – where English is spoken – is our love of football.'

- 'It is difficult to speak of a British culture because there are so many groups of different national and ethnic origins: African, Afro-Caribbean, Indian, Asian, East European and so on. They have their own national, ethnic, family and religious traditions.'

- 'A striking element of the culture of Northern Ireland is the historic hatred and violence between the Catholics and Protestants.'

- 'An important part of the Welsh culture is its language and its music.'

analyse this

Having studied the use of the word 'culture' in all four sentences you are now in a position to write your own definition of the word. What you will arrive at is a hypothetical definition of the word that can be tested and altered as you see more examples of its usage in this chapter. It is one of those complex words whose full meaning is not grasped until one has seen it used in different situations. Try writing it now in your note book.

■ Culture – an introduction

When speaking of a civilization, a nation, an ethnic group or a religion and various other types of groups, the word 'culture' includes all those

key terms

key terms

inductive learning

Learning by examining a number of examples and forming a general conclusion which applies to all of them. This is the basis of the scientific method, working from the particular to the general, forming a hypothesis for testing.

attributes that collectively help to describe that group. Thus we refer to the German culture, the French culture, the Chinese culture, the Welsh culture, the Muslim culture, the culture of the aborigines of Australia. The term includes customs, common knowledge, belief, attitudes and behaviour as represented in a variety of achievements and also in contemporary life. The past influences the present culture.

An easy description is to say that it is a way of life or a way of doing things, but if you think of a nation its culture will consist of many factors, including all or many of the following:

- history;
- education and language;
- values and attitudes;
- form of government and laws – democratic or dictatorial;
- systems and ways of doing things;
- customs, rituals and traditions;
- beliefs and behaviour;
- dress, food and ways of cooking;
- art, music and literature;
- sporting traditions.

Bonfires and fireworks on Guy Fawkes night are part of English culture. Under which of the headings in the above list do they come?

You will find other factors to add to the list, but when we use the word 'culture' we may use it in a more limited way that does not include all of these factors. It depends on the composition and size of the group being considered – a nation or a religion or a political party for example.

While you were studying Chapter 5 on different religions you probably became aware of cultural differences, even if the term did not occur to you.

High culture

This will be dealt with later in the chapter, but in case you come across it, here are a few words about it. We sometimes describe a person who is interested in and is knowledgeable about such things as music, opera, ballet, literature, art, theatre, architecture as being 'cultured' – 'high' or 'fine' culture includes all of those arts.

Pop culture

This will also be dealt with later in the chapter. Much pop culture is very accessible (easy to reach out to) and that is why it is popular.

If you need a quick reference, listen to Radio 1 for pop culture and Radio 3 for high culture.

Different national cultures

A way of trying to understand one's own national culture is to compare and contrast it with others on some of the important factors that make up the term 'culture'. Cultural differences are interesting in themselves, but comparisons with different cultures, as well as adding to our knowledge, can also increase our understanding of people of other nations.

We are often aware of these differences, although not in detail, and our limited knowledge may make us prejudiced. Do you think that the French culture is very different from ours?

- Does France have a monarchy?
- Is its system of government democratic?
- Is its major religion different from ours?
- Is it more of an industrial or more of an agricultural country?
- Is the population multi-ethnic?
- Is its cuisine (style of cooking and food) special to France?
- What kind of a reputation does it have in the arts?
- Does its position in Europe contribute to its culture?
- Are the French more romantic?
- Are their television programmes different in any way?
- Does it have a pop culture (including music) similar to ours?
- Does it have a free health service and state pensions?
- Is its education system like ours?

The Eiffel Tower, Paris

analyse this

Prepare a group presentation. Each member of the group should select one of the features listed above (the country does not have to be France) and do some research for a group presentation in which each student shows the similarities and differences between French and British (or English, Scottish, Welsh, Irish) cultures.

You can make a swift start by using a good encyclopedia but, if there is time, someone can write to the French Embassy in London for information. After every student has given her or his presentation someone should bring out the main points of the whole group exercise. What are the important cultural differences and similarities?

■ The influence of science and technology on culture

People's lives, and consequently the culture, have changed considerably thanks to scientific and technological development. Fifty years ago, in winter, most families sat round a coal fire at night listening to the 'wireless' (radio) and took a hot-water bottle to bed in a cold bedroom.

Nowadays most of them sit in a centrally heated room watching television and retire to a bed in a warm room, heated by an electric blanket. Washing machines, dish washers, tumble dryers, televisions, refrigerators and freezers, central heating, microwave ovens and all kinds of electrical gadgets have changed lives considerably since the 1950s, taking much of the drudgery out of family life, giving greater comfort and convenience, and leaving more time for leisure activities. Science and technology have made it that much easier for both husband and wife to go out to work.

The car and caravan have provided more opportunities for weekend outings and holidays. The mass of people in this country have much more varied lives.

Science has provided more cures, a popular one being knee or hip replacement. It has given us more information about healthy living and diet and the result is that people are living longer. We are going through a time when infertile couples are being helped to have babies by a variety of scientific techniques, including frozen embryos and *in vitro* fertilization. This makes for happy couples, but we cannot foresee what the future will bring in this field or the effect upon our culture. At the beginning of 2003 the ethics of human cloning – a possibility within reach of scientists – is exercising people's consciences.

Generally our lives are more varied, our interpersonal relationships are more about our interests and leisure activities and conversation is no longer about Monday washing and getting it dry and ironed with a flat iron heated on the gas stove.

■ Multi-ethnic Britain and the effect upon culture

analyse
this

Look at the following extracts taken from *The Economist*.

At the end of the street stands the church, its steeple rising high above the roofs of the neighbouring terraces. The roads on either side are named after English county *towns – Cambridge, Stafford, Warwick and so on – and in the pub on the corner of Warwick Street the pints are being pulled. Oh, to be in England.* But this is not quite the England of Robert Browning. This is Oldham, a decaying cotton town just out-side Manchester, where litter blows in the street, buddleia sprouts from the brick-work of the factories that made 19th century Lancashire rich – and the children running into the building opposite the pub are Muslims arriving for their daily meas-ure of Koranic instruction.*

Similar scenes can be found in many towns in Western Europe these days. It is hardly a novelty to see women in saris, men wearing turbans, or signs written in strange scripts.

(*Robert Browning's poem Home-Thoughts From Abroad)

(*The Economist*, 10 August 2002, Special Report, Muslims in Western Europe, 'Distant drums throbbing in the hills half heard.')

Question

Using the above extract write a paragraph or two showing why it is difficult to speak of one, unified British culture. Or make a list of all the examples of different ethnic origins you have seen, commenting on one or two of them. For example a Bollywood cinema, Chinatown or a kebab takeaway.

analyse
this

British culture and its subcultures

1 To begin, we should consider the expression 'subculture'. The word 'sub' does not mean inferior. It means existing within the mainstream culture. So we may speak of the Indian or Pakistani or Jewish or pop subculture existing within mainstream British culture.

2 Immigrants to this country may have particular reasons for coming here, for example economic or family reasons, but the majority of them come with a particular per-ception, or view, of Britain, which includes such concepts as:

- impartial justice and legal rights;

- a tradition of democratic government;

- equality of opportunity;

- respect for the person;

- healthcare;

- help for the poor;

- free education;

- freedom to worship according to one's own religion;

- a high degree of personal freedom;

- a highly developed level of the arts, entertainment and the media;

- a higher standard of living.

In other words they have expectations about the culture of Britain.

3 Whilst the majority of the British people of all ethnic origins would generally agree with the above description of British culture in principle, the ideals have not always worked out in practice and changes in the law have been needed to deal with racial prejudice, discrimination and intolerance by people, groups and institutions. Nonetheless, Britain is still a destination for immigrants, legal and illegal, which suggests that their perceptions of British culture are favourable in some ways.

4 *Acculturation* (adapting to other cultures). Immigration has led to some changes in the British way of life. There has been integration more or less of the different ethnic groups. Britain has grown more cosmopolitan (consisting of people from many parts of the world). There have been inter-racial marriages. Institutions have tried to adapt to the racial mix. Official forms are available in a variety of languages. Schools have developed multicultural education, and holidays are granted for all religious anniversaries and festivals, not just Christian.

5 About a quarter of nurses and doctors are from other countries or are of other ethnic origins. There are famous black footballers and Asian cricketers; well-known Asian and black newsreaders; and popular entertainers from all ethnic groups. There are mosques and temples in Britain, Chinese takeaways and curry houses. Most people know about Ramadan and Diwali and when to expect Chinese or Jewish New Year. And, although there has been inter-racial feuding, in many organizations people of different ethnic origins and religions work alongside each other. All this is natural now, but in total it represents an important change to the British culture since the 1950s, when immigration began on a large scale.

6 Where people's ethnic origins or traditions are different from the mainstream culture of the country they are living in they do, on the whole, try to involve themselves in the institutions and customs of the country, whilst maintaining their own cultures.

Muslims, for example, go to their mosque, buy meat from *halal* shops, avoid alcohol, oppose borrowing and lending money for interest and wear traditional dress. But they also use supermarkets and banks and read national newspapers. They are members of Parliament, chiefs of police, they sit on local councils and are involved in local joint initiatives. They own shops, which everyone uses, and run large corporations and for the most part watch the same TV programmes as the rest of the nation.

7 There are, however, some groups that try to maintain a high degree of separation from mainstream culture.

8 Strict, Orthodox Jews abide by religious commands that forbid them from taking anything out of their houses on the Sabbath. They may go to the synagogue, but strictly they are forbidden from taking with them anything from the house: no keys, no wheelchairs, no prams or pushchairs or other items, not even a prayer book when going to the synagogue. Driving a car is also forbidden. Where there are young children in a family it is difficult to go out without a pushchair or pram.

9 In north London an *eruv* is to be set up. An *eruv* is an area with a fixed boundary that, by custom, Jews are allowed to treat as their home for essential purposes. This means that they will be able to leave the house bringing with them essential items, but not leave the *eruv* with them. The area is about five square miles.

10 Natural boundaries such as roads and railways may form part of *eruv* boundaries, otherwise thin poles linked with fine wire, like a fishing line, are used. The wire will probably be about 6 metres high.

11 *Fundamentalism.* Orthodox Jews stick strictly to the Torah (the first five books of the Old Testament), following the laws about animals that may be eaten and ritual cleanliness, as set out in the book of Leviticus. In the synagogues prayers are said in Hebrew. As for the cultural aspect of orthodoxy, at home they may speak Yiddish or have a great deal of Yiddish in their conversation. Their cultural heritage expects that the men do not shave (Leviticus 19: 26) and will dress in black suits with coat tails and wear black hats. The women will wear dark dresses and hats or wigs. This dress tradition did not originate in the hot climate of the Jews' original home in the Middle East, but in cold central and eastern Europe, especially Poland, where it became a symbol of membership of their group and an outward sign of their serious religious intent.

12 This small group of Jews living in the wider culture of this country, earning a living, raising a family, using the modern utilities, including cars, computers and other facilities, is able to maintain its own religious, cultural heritage. We can speak quite definitely about an orthodox subculture, though the group would speak of *their way of life* rather than describe orthodoxy as a subculture.

key terms

Hebrew

An ancient name for the Jews and for their language.

Yiddish

A language developed by the Jews from a German dialect, used by them in central and eastern Europe. It includes some Hebrew words.

Questions

Here are some multiple-choice questions. In each case choose the best answer or answers from a, b, c and d.

1 According to the section above entitled 'British culture and its subcultures', which of the following is or are the main reasons for immigrants coming to this country?

   a for economic reasons;

   b to join their families;

   c to escape persecution;

   d for freedom.

2 In point 2 of the section which of the factors listed are likely to be legal rights?

   a a highly developed level of the arts, entertainment and the media;

   b respect for the person;

   c free education;

   d healthcare.

3 According to point 3 which of the following is true?

   a Most people would agree with the definition of British culture.

   b Some of the principles have had to be implemented by the law.

   c Britain is not a popular country for immigrants.

   d Immigrants have no idea about the British culture.

4 Points 4 and 5 say or imply which of the following statements?

   a Most hospital workers are black or Asian.

b People generally know very little about the culture of other religions or ethnic groups.

c People of different ethnic groups tend to have different jobs.

d Over the last 50 years British culture has changed because of the arrival of people of different cultures.

5 Which of the following statements is/are true, according to point 8?

a On the Sabbath, Orthodox Jews who want to leave the house cannot lock their front doors.

b People who cannot walk cannot leave their homes on the Sabbath, unless they are carried.

c Orthodox Jews must not leave their prayer books in the synagogue.

d They may take money to the synagogue on the Sabbath.

6 The purpose of an *eruv*, according to point 9, is which of the following?

a to separate the Jewish home from the synagogue;

b to separate Orthodox Jews from other people;

c to extend the area designated as the home;

d to mark out the territory of the Orthodox Jews.

7 Which of the following is true, according to point 11?

a An important idea in Jewish Orthodoxy is individual free will.

b Male Orthodox Jews dress in black, in accordance with the book of Leviticus.

c The women wear wigs to be stylish.

d None of the above, a, b or c, is true.

8 Which one of the following statements best describes the general approach of the section, 'British culture and its subcultures'?

a It shows a belief in the need for immigration.

b It expresses some doubt about whether immigration is good for Britain.

c It shows sympathy for people of different ethnic groups and religions.

d It tries to be factual, expressing no particular opinion on the subject of immigration.

Now that you have completed question number 8, write about three paragraphs explaining the reasons for your answer, using any examples from the section as illustration or proof of your statements.

analyse this

England

The following extract from *Notes From a Small Island* by Bill Bryson, an English-speaking American, shows how ignorant he was of our language and Englishness when he first arrived in England.

England was full of words I'd never heard before – streaky bacon, short back and sides, Belisha beacon, serviettes, high tea, ice-cream cornet. I didn't know how to pronounce 'scone' or 'pasty' or 'Towcester' or 'Slough'. I had never heard of Tesco's, Perthshire or Denbighshire, council houses, Morecambe and Wise, railway cuttings, Christmas crackers, bank holidays, seaside rock, milk floats, trunk calls, Scotch eggs, Morris Minors and Poppy Day. For all I knew, when a car had an L-plate on the back of it, it indicated that it was being driven by a leper . . .

I saw a man in a newsagent's ask for 'twenty Number Six' and receive cigarettes, and presumed for a long time afterwards that everything was ordered by number in a newsagent's, like in a Chinese takeaway. I sat for half an hour in a pub before I realized that you had to fetch your own order, then tried the same in a tea-room and was told to sit down.

Bill Bryson is not analysing the British culture, but he is pointing to some differences in word usage and customs between two English-speaking countries. Bill Bryson is an American; he speaks English, but he found some of our customs and language differences confusing.

The point about this extract is that it shows that there are things that we take for granted, which need no explanation, except to foreigners. This is an important aspect of one's culture, whether it be a national culture or a subculture: we take it for granted.

Question

In small groups do a spider diagram in which you think of:

- five or more American customs;

- uses of language which are different from ours.

Any American films that you have seen may help. Here's a start:

- The Americans celebrate Thanksgiving Day.

- Americans call a car boot 'a trunk' and refer to autumn as 'the Fall'.

Try to find out the origins of some of the customs.

The original Thanksgiving, in 1621

Language

An important question is that of language. Where families of different ethnic origins have their own language it is natural that they will want to keep it alive by using it. However, as English is the major language of this country it is also important that everyone is fluent in it – firstly, because it is a basic necessity if one is to venture outside the home, to attend school, to take a job and to find one's way around, but secondly because language is a bridge between races. Communication is important if people, their customs and religious practices are to be understood.

The British have a poor reputation for learning foreign languages compared with our continental neighbours. This failing is almost a part of our culture. One of the reasons for this is that we have been more isolated from other countries than other Europeans have, but also, during our history of empire building, English became what is called a *lingua franca,* a language commonly used by foreigners to converse with people of different languages. Consequently many English nationals rely upon people of other countries to speak English. If you go into a café in Paris and say 'un bier, s'il vous plâit', the waiter will probably respond with 'certainly, sir' or 'certainly, madam'.

analyse this

What follows is an extract from *The Economist*:

The immigrants who arrived in Oldham in the 1970s and 1980s came to work in the textile industry, expecting to go home to the Indian subcontinent in due course . . . But for most of them the return has never happened. Meanwhile, they have failed to learn English . . . very well and to make matters worse, most of their original jobs have gone. Now, in Oldham at least, any work to be had is in offices or banks or dry cleaners, where a command of the language is far more important than in a textile mill.

The article then goes on to say that the children of these immigrants have suffered in their education because they spoke their parents' language.

(The Economist, 10 August 2002, Special Report, Muslims in Western Europe, Distant drums throbbing in the hills half heard.')

Now consider the following two pieces of information:

- At a local Chinese fish and chip shop they all speak Chinese behind the counter but English when they are serving hungry customers.

- A Home Secretary has been criticised by civil and ethnic rights groups for saying that English should be developed and spoken in homes where families speak their own ethnic language.

Question

Take the above article and this advice by the Home Secretary and write about three paragraphs showing how language problems should be dealt with. Should immigrants who have little English be required to undergo lessons in spoken English? Should families be encouraged to use English in the home? Is one's ethnic language important for keeping alive one's ethnic culture?

The issues may seem clear, but they are also very sensitive. You could try to weigh up the advantages and disadvantages. If you speak only English you may be able to discuss the question with a fellow student whose home language is not English.

■ Language and ways of thinking

Language is an important and sophisticated way of communicating with other people, not only to understand them but to be able to talk to them. A vital function of language, often overlooked, is thinking. We think in language. In fact some behavioural psychologists believe that all thinking is talking, but we are not always aware of it because it is subvocal (not spoken aloud). With language we can solve problems, consider alternative solutions, analyse complicated ideas and so on. Language more than assists our understanding; it is the *means* of understanding. With limited language an individual is limited in the kind of thought processes he or she can use.

analyse this

different ways of thinking

Ways of thinking can vary according to one's culture. Where this is so it needs to be fully understood and taken into consideration when people of different cultures are striving to communicate.

A Chinese psychologist at the University of California examined 500 students in China and America, and Patricia McBroom in her paper 'American and Chinese have different ways of discovering truth' reports on some interesting comparisons between the Chinese and the American ways. For example, Americans, in any argument, desperately need to find out who is right whereas the Chinese are 'far more content to think that both sides have flaws and virtues'. The Chinese are more likely to look for compromise, to seek the middle way. In studies of argument between people, for example between mother and daughter, Americans blamed one side, usually the mother, for causing the problems and offered no compromise in trying to solve them. The Chinese sought compromise, blaming no one, trying to bring both sides together. Even in tests of scientific thinking, Chinese students took the middle way. Asked a question of scientific fact, such as 'does smoking cause weight gain or loss?' the Chinese 'took the middle road' even after reading the evidence and actually believing one statement to be less true than another.

Peng, the Chinese psychologist who carried out this research, says that Americans 'seek the right and wrong answers and tend to become even more convinced of the rightness of their position after reading a counter-argument'. Peng concludes that 'life is full of contradictions and the best way is to use both styles of thinking and responding, one for science and another for relationships' – clear, direct linear thinking for science and the middle road compromise for relationships. (Patricia McBroom's report dated 6 September 1998 can be seen in full at www.berkeley.edu/news/media/releases.)

Where there are such differences in their ways of thinking, people of different cultures will be on different 'wavelengths' and find it hard to understand the other person's position.

Questions

1 Which of the following is most likely to be true, according to Peng?

a The Americans' ways of thinking are more likely to produce solutions to problems.

b Chinese thinking is more effective in dealing with science problems.

c In human relations and in science the Chinese way of thinking is more appropriate.

d The American thinking finds it difficult to balance opposing arguments between people and tends to support one side or the other.

2 Which of the following statements best sums up the above paragraph?

a The Chinese and the Americans both have the same ways of discovering the truth.

b After listening to opposite views to their own, the Americans are more likely to be convinced by the opposite views.

c The Chinese need to think logically in science, searching for the solution to a problem and the Americans need to seek compromise in matters of relationships between people.

d In arguments between people the Americans seek to bring both sides together.

Language and culture are mutually influential

Language and culture influence each other. Writers, for example, are guided by the cultural customs and taboos (restrictions) of their times, but they can take the risk of trying to change them. D.H. Lawrence's novel *Lady Chatterley's Lover,* written in 1928, was banned in this country because Lawrence used four-letter Anglo-Saxon sexual words. The words were known, but the existing cultural customs suppressed them as vulgar and obscene and writers kept to the social restrictions when writing about sex if they wanted their books published.

In a celebrated court case in 1960 *Lady Chatterley' s Lover* was approved for publication. The court verdict brought in a new age of freedom of expression. Since that time there has been hardly any restriction on writers or film and TV programme makers; witness the 2002 film, *Bridget Jones's Diary*. The whole range of once-forbidden words simply tumbled out of the censor's box enabling generations of young people to hear, accept, even use them, with nothing like the shock and horror of their parents or grandparents. The words can, of course, still cause offence and may be taboo in some subcultures, but our cultural mores (moral customs) have opened up to these words and, some would argue, have given more precision to the language. (There is a section on censorship in Chapter 10.)

Sex and culture

Since about the same time as the *Lady Chatterley* case there has been a growing change in society's attitude towards sex and sexual relations. Naturally, sexual intercourse took place outside marriage and there were gay relationships centuries before this time – read about the Greeks – but the subject and talk about it became less of a taboo from the 1960s.

The national culture has had to adapt to changes in sexual attitudes as homosexuality between consenting adults is no longer illegal, as more and more people live together without marrying, and as more and more people are engaging in casual sexual activity. In the 1960s condoms were kept under chemists' counters. From the early 1980s they started to appear on supermarket shelves.

The interest in all this is not, of course, sex itself, but the dramatic change that has taken place in an important aspect of human relations and consequently in our national culture over the last 40 years or more. So much is now taken for granted that at one time caused shock and embarrassment.

This is not to suggest that free sexual relations are to be encouraged or approved. Some parents do not approve of all the activities of their offspring; they just accept what goes on.

It is interesting that whereas the national culture has come to accept this greater freedom and tolerance, in many religious and ethnic subgroups there is strong opposition to sex outside marriage and to homosexuality.

The point about this is that we take our culture for granted, but are not always aware that culture is dynamic – that it changes and that there are often different views between subgroup cultures and the mainstream culture.

analyse
this
culture changes

The following extract is taken from the New Zealand writer, Margaret McLaren's book *Interpreting Cultural Differences*:

Culture is not fixed. Dress, food, housing, attitudes to inheritance, sex, marriage, health, education and many other matters change. In a western community it now seems extraordinary that two centuries ago possessions passed normally only to male members of a family, and a married woman had no income of her own. Even fifty years ago, it was exceptional for a man and woman to live together outside marriage in a western community.

Twenty years ago in New Zealand the hosts' first job after a party was to open all the windows to get rid of the cigarette smoke. Now it is rare for anyone to smoke inside someone else's house, at least without specially asking for, and being given, permission.

Within a culture, variation occurs. Subcultures, or groups similar in age, education, wealth, interests, sports and many other factors, may exist within a larger culture. Most people belong to more than one subculture, even in a foreign country.

analyse
this
an old advertisement for cigarettes

The advertisement that appears on page 69 is taken from *Picturegoer,* the national film weekly for the week ending 24 July 1954.

In the past, smoking has been advertised as safe, healthy, beautifying, likely to improve your social and sex life as well as having many other desirable effects. In films from the 1940s and 1950s nearly every character smoked. It was thought sophisticated. Lady Bracknell, in Oscar Wilde's play *The Importance of Being Earnest* (produced in 1895), approved of Ernest's smoking because she thought that every young gentleman should have a hobby!

Look at the advertisement from 1954 opposite and state what qualities are suggested as being linked with smoking these cigarettes.

Picture Post, 9 January, 1954

What might David Niven be doing?

At the moment, he's in the studio, making a phone call — or, more accurately, making a phone call the excuse to sit down for a moment and enjoy a much needed cigarette.

What he *might* be doing is another story. The fact is, he does so many things, there's no knowing what he might be doing if you met him off parade (as they used to say when he was a regular officer in a Highland regiment).

But whatever he's doing — water ski-ing or spear-fishing off the Californian coast, playing golf at St. Andrews or painting pictures in Oxfordshire — you can be sure of one thing. There'd be a packet of Capstan in the picture.

"Well, naturally," he says. "Whatever I do, I must have a cigarette. Won't you?"

Have a CAPSTAN

—they're made to make friends

★ DAVID NIVEN stars with Yvonne de Carlo and Barry Fitzgerald in Mario Zampi's gay Associated British Technicolor comedy—"O'Leary Night".

W. D. & H. O. Wills, Branch of The Imperial Tobacco Company (of Great Britain & Ireland), Ltd.   CC837M

Smoking and the cultural change

Changed attitudes to smoking since the 1950s represent a considerable variation in the culture of this country. Smoking in now generally thought to be anti-social for it is banned in many places where people get together, and if it is not banned, smokers and non-smokers are segregated (set apart).

Smoking and cancer

In the 1960s it was confirmed that smoking was linked to cancer. Some years afterwards there was a ban on television advertising and a statutory health warning began to appear on all tobacco products.

analyse this

Which of the following 10 warnings do you think have appeared on cigarette packets and posters?

1 Smoking causes heart disease.

2 Chief Medical Officers' warning.

3 12 mg Tar 1.0 mg Nicotine.

4 Protect children: don't make them breathe your smoke.

5 Smoking when pregnant harms your baby.

6 Smoking causes cancer.

7 Smoking causes fatal diseases.

8 Low tar is safer.

9 Smoking will cause your death.

10 Smoke less: live longer.

It was a peculiar contradiction that advertisements to encourage smoking carried such warnings.

Advertising ban

At midnight on 13 February 2003 all advertising for, and promotion and sponsoring by, tobacco products was banned, with a few exceptions such as advertising on the shelves of shops selling tobacco and cigarettes. Tobacco sponsoring of global sports such as snooker and Formula One racing is exempt from the ban until July 2006.

During the days before the ban came into force, some of the advertisers had a final fling. One cigarette company produced a colour giveaway sheet which was a pictorial history of their amusing advertisements. Another company, advertising cigars, did something similar and ended its handout with the following lament: 'Sod's law decrees Hamlet moments will never end (shame our ads have to stop)'.

Within one week of the ban on tobacco advertising Dot, a popular and religious character on the soap *Eastenders*, was seen to smoke a cigarette. She regularly does so in the series! Could this be seen as unintentional promotion of smoking?

It is a sobering thought that, according to the Chief Executive of Cancer Research, UK, about 450 British children start smoking every day. And the British Medical Association reports that about 1000 people a day are dying from passive smoking. It calls for a ban on smoking in all public places. As harmful as it may be, smoking itself is not banned, nor is it likely to be in any democratic country, but our government hopes, even expects, that banning advertising will result in a reduction in smoking and a reduction of about 3000 deaths per year.

Smoke-free zones began to spread rapidly from about the mid-1990s and there are now very few public places where people may smoke. In the 1950s cinema audiences watched film stars smoke on the silver screen and as they did so the audience themselves smoked and stubbed out their cigarettes on ashtrays fixed to the back of the seats in front of them. If you looked up to the ceiling you saw great clouds of smoke drifting through the beam which projected the film on to the screen. Now, smoking in cinemas and theatres and in many shops is banned. When shops banned smoking it gave rise to a very peculiar habit or custom. More and more shop assistants have since been seen outside shopping malls, in town streets, standing in doorways and on pavements, putting up with the wind and rain, in order to smoke a cigarette during their breaks.

A competition to coin a name for these outside smokers came up with some interesting suggestions, including 'snoutcasts', 'snout' being prison slang for tobacco or cigarettes. Look for the word in new editions of dictionaries. Spike Milligan, zany comedian and anti-smoking campaigner, once suggested that in order to prevent passive smoking, smokers in buildings should be made to wear a great funnel over their heads while smoking. On top of the funnel would be a wide pipe to carry the smoke through the roof to the outdoors! Spike was not only zany, he had a wry sense of humour.

It is not surprising that some smokers are paranoid (feeling persecuted).

This variation in our culture began with statistical and scientific evidence showing the dangers of smoking. The change in attitude and in social behaviour has come about through the actions of pressure groups such as ASH (Action on Smoking and Health), medical research and the actions of governments.

But, of course, there are many people who still smoke, either because they choose to do so or because although they would like to give it up, they find it difficult to do so. Do smokers have a sense of persecution? Shouldn't they be allowed to carry on smoking without being made to feel immoral, injurious to others, and scapegoats? How harmful is smoking compared with excessive consumption of alcohol or drug-taking?

key terms

Passive smoking

The inhaling by non-smokers of other popele's smoke when in the same room as smokers.

Sod's law

A pessimistic view that if there is any chance of the worst thing happening, it will always happen.

analyse this

Using the sections on 'Culture changes', the old cigarette advert and 'Smoking and cultural change', write about 350 words on smoking, covering the following points. Remember to consider opposing views, and to express your own views clearly and with reasons.

1 The change in attitudes to smoking and in behaviour since the 1960s. Reasons for the change.

2 The rights of smokers. Freedom of the individual. Tolerance.

3 Smokers are becoming a persecuted group.

4 The question of smoking as a health problem for smokers and passive smokers.

5 Whether any further action needs to be taken either to restrict smoking or to restore rights to smokers.

6 Should smoking on all television productions be banned because it promotes the habit as much as advertising did, or should it be allowed to continue for the sake of realism?

(The government claims vast sums of money from duty on all tobacco goods.)

Questions

Use the sections on 'Culture changes' and 'an old advertisement for cigarettes' to help you with the following questions.

1 Interview someone over the age of 40 years. It could be your parents, relations, family friends or a teacher, to find out what cultural changes have taken place in their lifetime. Work out 10 questions or more (in discussion groups, if you wish). It is surprising how many adults like to do a recorded interview. Then write a 350-word report on the interview in which you highlight the changes, and comment upon them.

2 Alternatively, do a class presentation of your findings.

The case studies will give you some ideas and here are some suggested questions:

- What was it like when you went to school?

- How has family life changed?

- What changes have taken place in work patterns?

- What differences are there in people's leisure and cultural activities?

analyse this

Asian and Australian students – differences in attitudes and customs

This case study gives a comparison between some aspects of Asian and Australian cultures. It is a series of extracts from *Boomerang Magazine, the Voice of International Students in Australia*. In these extracts students compare and contrast Asian values and customs with those of Australia. They are followed by some multiple-choice questions.

1 The Asian students who spoke to *Boomerang* found that there are differences between the value systems but slowly these are shifting.

2 Study and examinations – one immediate example of differences is the relaxed attitude to study by Australian students. Hui Li, a Singaporean computing student at Monash University, finds that generally, Australian students are more relaxed about their workload. 'Study is very important to Asian students,' she says, 'Australian students make sure they achieve their goal but they don't necessarily aim for the highest mark. But Asians want to be the best. Plus Australians seem to be more open to different ways of learning and more flexible, which Asians may not be.'

3 Boon Keong thinks, 'There is a tendency for Asian students to be more competitive while Aussies seem to take things at their own pace and be more relaxed.'

4 Money – Moulisa, a Malaysian-Indian, believes, 'Australians tend to start work at a younger age, often doing part-time work while still in high school to earn some extra pocket money . . . But the Asian way is to study hard, work hard, make money, forget about having fun and save your dollars for your unborn children . . . the purpose of career and money is not only to provide, but it's also a status thing.'

5 Jehn, a Singaporean student, believes that the importance of looking after family members stems from the days when Asian families were very large. 'With bigger families you have limited resources, which leads to a greater emphasis on getting money and material goods. In Australia the population is generally smaller, with seemingly enough land and resources for everybody.'

6 Joseph, an Australian student doing Psychology at Monash says, 'We're a bit more relaxed about almost everything, so that also goes for money and career . . . money is just the means to an end; something that enables me to lead a life that is comfortable'.

7 Courtship and marriage – Asians also seem to have more traditional views and expectations about family and relationships. Moulisa says, 'After I finish my post-graduate study I'll probably get married, and yeah, it will be arranged. I'll have a choice of which guy I want to marry, of course, but it's definitely not going to be a Western-style courtship.'

8 'Arranged marriages are not as common as they used to be; I know lots of Indian girls who aren't going to do it. And I don't think my mum and dad want me to support

them in old age either. Hui Li says, 'There's still a bit of stigma (about divorce) and for some it may be a disgrace, . . . but I think nowadays it's more up to the people themselves . . . Aussies find it easier to divorce than we do.'

9 Parental control – Joseph (Australian student) says, 'Australians tend to have more lenient interaction (with their parents). Most people I know are fairly free, but there are some Australian parents who are quite controlling of their kids.'

10 For Jehn, respect and care of his parents are very big issues. 'In Asia, parents are the greater authority. As a child, you love your parents, but you are still very scared of them . . . for Australians and other Westerners, the relationship is similar to a contract. Like, if you don't clean your room, you can't watch TV. For us, if we don't clean our room, it's a sign of disrespect that we haven't obeyed our parents.'

11 Religious freedom – 'Asia has more gods,' Joseph exclaims. 'I think it's cool how there are so many religions in Asia and they accept the presence of one another. With traditional Anglo-Saxon religion, the dominant presence is Christianity and its various spin-offs. The message is "You have to believe us and nobody else."'

12 Changing values. The article ends ups with a summary which, referring to 'these shifting times', thinks that for Australians, individual choice is an important factor, whereas in Asia, one has to take family and tradition into consideration. These notions are beginning to become unstuck, and signs of change are becoming apparent. The editor has noticed on campus Asian students with hair 'dyed blonde, striking purple and even Day-Glo orange.' Just one of the reasons for concluding that East and Wests are merging.

More detail can be found at www.boomerangmagazine.com.au.

Questions

1 According to points 2 and 3, which of the following statements, a , b, c or d, best describes the students?

a Australian students seldom achieve their goals.

b Asian students aim to get the best results.

c Both Asian and Australian students try to get the best mark in examinations.

d Asian and Australian attitudes to study are about the same.

2 Which of the following statements is true, according to points 3, 4 and 5?

a Asian students tend to spend money easily.

b Money is more important to the Asians.

c   Asian students want to make money for the future.

d   Australians are more concerned about their careers.

3 Points 7 and 8: which of the following statements does the research seem to be making?

a   All Asian students come from a strictly traditional background.

b   All Asian parents expect that in their old age their children will support them.

c   Some of the Asian traditions are gradually changing.

d   Divorce is acceptable in Asian society.

4 After studying points 9 and 10 choose the best answer from the following.

a   The relationship between children and parents is much the same for Asians as it is for Australians.

b   Asians tend to love and respect their parents more than the Australians do theirs.

c   Asian parents are more authoritative.

d   Australian parents trust their children more than Asian parents trust their children.

5 According to paragraphs 11 and 12, which of the following statements is most accurate?

a   In Asia there is little religious tolerance.

b   In Asia there is no individual choice.

c   There are indications among the Asian students that they are beginning to free themselves from their own cultural background.

d   There are indications among all students that they are beginning to free themselves from their own cultural backgrounds.

6 Using the case study write about 300 to 350 words on some of the difficulties that students studying in a different culture may experience.

■ High culture

You may sometimes hear of a person being referred to as 'cultured', which generally means that he or she enjoys the ballet or the opera or symphony

concerts, or visits art galleries or is immersed in literature. The expression 'high culture' is used to refer to the arts, music, performing arts and literature.

They are an important representational part of a national culture and it is often from these that we appreciate something of a different culture. The small principality of Wales is well-known in particular for its music and choirs, Scotland for its kilts and bagpipes, Austria for Strauss's waltzes, Milan for its opera, Moscow for its prestigious ballet school, (the Bolshoi), France for its nineteenth-century artists and the impressionist school of painting, and so on.

analyse this

What is Britain noted for? Think about it and then make some notes. Your list may include Shakespeare's works, London theatres, the Beatles and so forth.

■ Pop culture

Pop culture is often looked down upon by the experts of high culture for it is seen by some of them as inferior, less demanding, less intellectual, having little artistic merit and to be unlikely to last for long.

The main difference between high and pop culture is that the latter reaches many more people. You can see why. Most of the music which is generally popular is much easier to listen to – it is not so intellectually demanding, is generally accompanied by striking videos and can be enjoyed whilst doing other things. Much of the 'high culture' music – that of Mozart, Beethoven, Elgar, Benjamin Britten for example – does not appeal immediately and requires intensive listening for longer spells at a time.

Is it more meaningful? Only if you think so. For many people such music is meaningless. Much of high culture, including music, literature and the arts, tends to be more formal, with more rules, though not so much during the latter part of the twentieth century. Pop culture tends to be freer and looser in expression, sometimes promoting a kind of teenage rebellion.

The term 'pop' has become linked with 'teenage culture', perhaps because of such programmes as *Top of the Pops,* which has a young following. This encourages a kind of devotion to pop stars, pop groups and 'bands' who can fill stadiums and farmers' fields with cheering, waving supporters, as keen to join in as to listen to the music. By comparison, symphonic concerts, opera and ballet are held in concert halls and opera houses and,

although they rouse the emotions of the audience, the people generally contain themselves until the end of a performance. Pop music encourages people to display their feelings instantly and vigorously; vocally and physically.

As is often the case, we speak in general terms, for it is not always easy to categorize any art form. The Beatles were champions of pop, but they are hard to place. Some of their music has been played by symphony orchestras; they appeal to a very wide and mixed audience and their recordings are frequently played today, 35 or more years later.

Questions

1 List as many things as you can think of that are part of pop culture. Your list may include 'discos' and 'clubbing'.

2 Discuss, in a small group, one of the following statements to help you to put into perspective what is often a kind of rivalry between high and pop cultures. Try to present both sides of the picture.

- High culture tends to be more intellectual. Pop culture is more emotional.

- Pop culture is more important because it appeals to far more people than high culture.

- It is impossible to show that one culture is superior to another because they are so different.

- There is some beautiful singing in opera. The trouble is that it looks silly when performers sing while they're dying.

- Some of the lyrics of pop songs and albums are weak and silly.

- Can people appreciate all cultures, enjoying pop music as well as symphonies?

- Many classics have been made into popular works, for example *West Side Story* is based on Shakespeare's *Romeo and Juliet* and *Kiss me Kate* on his *Taming of the Shrew.* Why bother with the classics when modern versions are more real and more easily understood?

- If the works of high culture are so important why don't they reach out to the majority of the people?

3   After your discussions write about 350 words on one of the following, remembering the advice at the end of Chapter 1. Evidence and illustration are needed.

- Explain and comment upon the differences between high and pop culture.

- British 'soaps', such as *Eastenders* and *Coronation Street*, are realistic and teach us about life and relationships with other people. Discuss this.

- The trouble with some pop music is that it is aimed at younger people and often seems childish. Do you agree?

- On the whole, classical music is bound to be superior to pop music because the composers and performers are always trained musicians. The pop music scene is full of amateurs.

- All art, music, literature and performing arts (stage, film and television) should entertain or appeal rather than educate. Discuss this. You may consider one or more of the four types of artwork given.

At the end of this chapter you now understand what culture means and the variety of ways in which it may be used. You also have an appreciation of the kinds of differences that exist between cultures.

Did you know?

- The Chinese colour for mourning is white!

- In Amsterdam there are coffee shops where drugs may be bought and smoked legally.

- The Japanese word for our favourite cold treat is *aisukuriimu*.

7

The role of the artist in society

This chapter begins by comparing the conditions of the artist in a dictatorship with those in a democracy and tries to understand artists by considering their creative role and what guides them in this role. The influences are personal and social. In considering artists' purposes we are really examining why they became artists in the first place.

The chapter continues by questioning whether the arts should have a purpose and therefore whether the artists should have a role. Should art teach – have a message for humanity – or should art be at the whim of the artist? A couple of surprising works of art are described, one from 1917 and the other from 2002, both of which may have been just a fancy of the artist. One thing seems very clear and that is that artists need to feel that they have an 'audience'.

The role of the artist in society was more controlled when the artist served religion, producing art whose purpose was to instruct people in the ways of righteousness. During the thirteenth to the sixteenth centuries artists may have served the Church but this did not prevent them from producing some magnificent works, a particular example of which is Michelangelo's painting of the Sistine Chapel in Rome.

An important social role of artists has been to provide us with a historical record from times before photography was invented. In some cases it was the intention of the artist to record some important event in history, but many a painting of people, buildings, courtyards has *incidentally* provided records of the times. Preserving something of a past time may not have been a role that the artist assumed but it is a role which posterity (following generations) has given to the artist.

In the case study about didactic art the point is made that artists, like anyone else, have views about society and politics, the implication being that such views are likely to inform their works.

This is followed by a feature on modern, conceptual art, including some of the exhibits for the Turner Prize, and the controversy they have generated. It is difficult to explain the role of the modern artist in society because society does not have the cohesion of previous centuries and artists now grapple with abstract ideas, seeing themselves as engaged in experiments. More than ever we rely upon, to put it simply, the artist's inclination.

Throughout this chapter the expression 'the arts' refers to painting, sculpture, architecture, music, literature and the performing arts. The word 'art' includes painting and sculpture.

◼ Artists in dictatorships and democracies

Artists in a dictatorship

In dictatorships the arts normally have to serve the government. In Nazi Germany, for example, all Jewish works were banned and only those works that supported Hitler's views were tolerated. Hitler praised the works of the German composer Wagner (1813–33) because he believed him to be anti-Semitic and because the northern mythology of Wagner's operas related to German folklore. The music was, therefore, considered to be nationalistic – Germanic. The role of the artist in Nazi Germany was to glorify the state.

Artists in democracies

In democratic countries the arts are free of political control but does that mean that the artist has no social role and the arts have no purpose other than to serve the artist's wishes and stimulate the viewer, the reader or the listener?

Artists of all kinds will want to stimulate their viewers, readers and listeners; they will want to generate new ideas and to add to the body of art but, unless the artist is wealthy, he or she has to take note of what the buying public wants.

◼ The creative role of artists

What is it that influences, guides and directs the artist when he or she is in a creative role? By 'creative role' is meant all the conditions that motivate the artist to begin to paint, sculpt, design, compose and so on. It starts with the new creative idea, sometimes incompletely formed, followed by emotion, mood and intellect, often accompanied by a sense of urgency to begin. He or she picks up the brush, the chisel, the music manuscript, and is in the creative role. It is a very personal experience.

The new idea and the creation depend upon some complex factors, which may be divided into the personal and the social, as follows:

Personal

- beliefs;

- emotions;

- intellect;

- purpose;

- sensitivity;

- breadth of vision;

- skill.

Social

- whether the state is democratic or dictatorial;

- its historical background;

- the social culture and mores (important customs);

- current schools of art, forms and fashions.

The artist does not exist in a vacuum. He is aware of society and social conditions, but he or she may be influenced positively or negatively by society. In other words, the artist may conform or rebel against not only social convention but against society itself.

■ The artist's purpose

Why does any artist begin a work of art or perform a work of art? Here are some obvious reasons:

- to produce something of beauty;

- to express a strong emotion;

- to express strong beliefs;

- to teach, persuade or influence;

- to commemorate something or someone;

- to serve an inner need to create

- to produce something new.

These are actually the reasons why someone wants to be an artist in the first place.

Young people – and not only they – go off to drama college determined to become actors, singers and dancers. Yet at any one time, at a conservative guess, 70 per cent of all actors are unemployed and, unless they have made their fortune, they take up any work that is going. What is it they are supposed to say when not acting? 'I'm between jobs, darling!' Why do they do it? For most of the reasons listed above. This is the pull that the art has over them.

Artists of all kinds have other purposes, too. They also work to earn money.

The lists above may not be complete, but they go a long way towards setting out the aims, if not the purpose, of the artist.

To conclude this section, see what Henri Matisse (1869–1954) had to say:

> When I started to paint, I felt transported into a kind of paradise . . . In everyday life, I was usually bored and vexed by the things that people were always telling me I must do. Starting to paint, I felt gloriously free, quiet, and alone.
> (Source: I. Chilvers, (1999) *A Dictionary of Twentieth-Century Art*, OUP, London.)

See www.stevedenning.com/Art_painting%20.html for different views on art and painting.

analyse this

Using what you have read so far, write about 300 words in which you discuss whether or not there is something special about the artist compared with other workers. You may choose one particular type of art if you wish.

Should the arts have a purpose and therefore the artists a role? Should the arts teach or be edifying in some way? Should all art be didactic (instructional) or should the approach be one of 'art for art's sake'? Artists of all kinds could argue that having to be didactic would cramp their imagination and creativity. On the other hand, art for art's sake could mean 'anything goes' and the public would be at the mercy of the artist's fancy.

Was it a case of fancy or whim with the artist Marcel Duchamp when, in 1917, he got hold of a porcelain urinal from a plumber's shop and offered it at an art exhibition in Paris, calling it *The Fountain*. His justification of it as a work of art was that it is not the creation that is important, but the *selection,* the *choice* of object. So there you are. If you have an old dustbin or an abandoned kitchen sink in your back garden you may fancy your chances!

It does not do to be flippant about art, though. It's a serious business; a very important world of thought, imagination and artistic skill. But we do not want to be fooled either! Here is another interesting case. The *Sun* newspaper of 19 October 2002 gave a report on what happened to a 'creation' by the artist Damien Hirst:

An art gallery cleaner binned a £5,000 work by Damien Hirst because he mistook it for rubbish. Emmanuel Asare spotted the pile of full ashtrays, beer bottles, cola tins, coffee cups and sweet wrappings – and thought it was leftovers from a party.

Hirst, 35, who shot to fame after pickling a sheep in formaldehyde, claimed the heap of rubbish represented his messy studio.

Does this also give you ideas?

According to Herbert Read (1972) art is a:

desire to please . . . Man responds to the shape and surface and mass of things present to his senses and that certain arrangements in the proportion of the shape and surface and mass of things result in pleasurable sensations.

analyse this

Discuss the following in a small group. 'The purpose behind Damien Hirst's collage of leftovers seems to be self-expression; it seems to be saying, "this is what I am like and I want people to know it."'

What do you think about this? How far do you think this is true of artists?

analyse this

didactic art

1 Didactic art is born of strongly held feelings and deep thoughts about the state of the world and the people in it. Such art is universal rather than national. A good example of didactic art is religious art, which can convey the passion of Christ's suffering and emphasize the meaning of His crucifixion, or which can frighten the world into goodness by depicting the horrors of hell. In the past, art and religion have worked hand in hand, with art providing the symbols and the illustration of religious texts and beliefs, although the best religious art goes beyond mere illustration, providing something of beauty, something edifying for all.

2 Albert Elsen in *Purposes of Art* (1962) is very positive about Christian art being propaganda. 'Since its inception [beginning]', he writes, 'Christian art has had the function of propaganda; in fact, it can be contended that all religious art serves the purpose of propaganda. "Propaganda" is to be here interpreted as the dissemination [spreading] of religious information and views through the medium of art.'

3 In this case the role of the artist is made clear. He or she serves religion, carries out a commission for it, or obeys orders, like the artists in Nazi Germany. In such situations the artist may or may not be in sympathy with the message. Another kind of didacticism is more subtle, more in keeping with the artist's own feelings. This distinction will become clearer when you read about Rembrandt's painting in point 5.

4 You have only to visit the National Gallery in London or a gallery near you to get some idea of how extensively the artist from the thirteenth century to the end of the sixteenth century was at the service of religion in Europe. In the National Gallery you will find, for example, the *Wilton Diptych*. This is like a double, folding photograph frame. The left side of the diptych shows King Richard II with two earlier kings and John the Baptist, who baptized Christ. The right-hand side shows the Virgin Mary, the boy Jesus and heavenly angels. This religious work, meant to stand on an altar for the King's private prayers, was painted about 1395, artist unknown.

5 In the same gallery you will find Rembrandt's painting of 1644, *Woman Taken in Adultery*. This painting captures the story of a woman who was brought to Christ for punishment by stoning to death. It is told in St. John's Gospel, Chapter 8. Christ says to the crowd; 'Whichever one of you has committed no sin may throw the first stone at her.' Completed over 200 years after the *Wilton Diptych* it is altogether a more human work, not about majesty and heaven but about forgiveness. As such it is universal; it is for all humanity.

6 One of the great religious works is the painted ceiling of the Sistine Chapel in Rome. Michelangelo (1475–1564), a sculptor, was persuaded by Pope Julius II, against his will, to paint vast frescoes on this ceiling. This great work, which took from 1508 until 1512, shows God's creation of man, paintings of prophets and scenes from the Bible. He took on the work after great pressure from the Pope, but it came from his own inspiration. He rejected the Pope's plans for the ceiling and presented his own. He chose to work mainly alone and painted in cramped conditions on top of the scaffolding, just below the ceiling, sometimes painting whilst lying on his back.

7 Painters were not the only artists at the service of religion. Architects and builders created great cathedrals and churches and artists filled them with paintings and sculptures. Oratorios and cantatas were composed to attract people to church and for our legacy we have Bach's cantatas and his St Matthew and St John Passions. From Handel we have *The Messiah* and *The Creation*. Up until the end of the fourteenth century medieval drama, which was a cycle of biblical plays, was performed in churches, but the plans were taken over by the craft guilds and performed in public places. Although they dealt with the seriousness of Christ's Passion, many of them were comic and they had the advantage over the Latin service of being in the language of the people.

8 Although most European art between the time of the painting of the *King Richard Diptych* and the *Woman Taken in Adultery* was religious, artists were often commissioned by wealthy patrons to paint their portraits and family groups. In this activity the role of the artist was to serve his patron and to produce a historical record for the patron and his family. Societies also commissioned work. Rembrandt did a painting of Professor Tulp's anatomy lesson.

9 From about the middle of the sixteenth century art became more secular, less grand in subject and broader in scope. The Dutch artist Jan Steen (1625–79) was painting his *Skittle Players Outside an Inn,* Vermeer (1632–75) was doing his domestic interiors, and Canaletto (1697–1768) was producing spectacular scenes of Venice. For the most part, artists relied upon commissions to make their living, but they were acquiring greater freedom of choice in subject matter and their role was changing.

10 Note the change that has taken place. You would hardly see an example of such ordinary domesticity in previous centuries. Contrast Vermeer's *Kitchen Maid* with Leonardo da Vinci's classic, relaxed beauty, the *Mona Lisa* – not a pot in sight. She is set in a haunting landscape, which echoes her wistfulness. Both can be seen in the coloured illustrations in Chapter 9.

Questions

Here are some multiple-choice questions on the case study. Study question number 1 carefully. It is not a trick question. You have to deduce (work out) the answer. (As a general rule do not fall into the trap of thinking that because any of the alternatives, a, b, c or d contain words or expressions used in the passage that must be the correct answer. Look for meaning and what is suggested.) When you have attempted the question, study the comments and answer given at the end of these questions. Then go on to do the rest of the questions.

1 The meaning of point 1 is that Christian art is an example of didactic art because:

a it is created from strong feelings;

b it is universal;

c it seeks to teach the Christian message;

d art and Christianity have worked hand in hand.

(Now see the comments after question number 8.)

2 In point 2 the author uses the word 'propaganda' to show which of the following?

a that religious art gives out a false message;

b how religious art can be misrepresented;

c that religious art sends out a message;

d his feelings about Christianity.

3 According to point 3:

  a didactic art can express the feelings of the artist;

  b the artist is independent;

  c artists in Nazi Germany served religion;

  d the artist was always in sympathy with the message he had to convey.

4 Point 4 shows:

  a that the *King Richard Diptych* was painted in the fifteenth century;

  b that the *Diptych* carried a painting showing two kings;

  c the purpose of the *Diptych*;

  d that the artist was at the service of religion for 400 years.

5 Point 6 suggests that:

  a Michelangelo was not keen to paint the ceiling because he was a sculptor;

  b he was opposed to doing the ceiling because he would have to work on his own;

  c Michelangelo resisted painting the ceiling at first because it would take too long to do;

  d he refused the work at first because painting the ceiling would be a back-breaking job.

6 According to point 7, which of the following is true?

  a The author suggests that the religious music is like a gift which was left for future generations.

  b The only arts that served religion were architecture, painting and music.

  c The medieval drama was in Latin.

  d Bach composed *The Messiah*.

7 The word 'secular' in point 9 shows which of the following?

  a That art was becoming more religious.

  b That art was freeing itself from religious propaganda.

  c That art was becoming more worldly, less spiritual.

  d That art was becoming less grand.

8   Which do you think is the most accurate statement about this article?

a   It is critical of didacticism in art.

b   It is in favour of didactic art.

c   It shows some different ways in which art can spread the Christian message.

d   It contains contradictions.

Here are some comments on the possible answers to question 1.

Answer a – be careful. The passage does use the expression 'strongly held feelings'. This is a feature of all didactic art, religious and otherwise; but that is not why Christian art is an example of didactic art.

Answer b – like a, the question uses a word from the text, 'universal'. Didactic art may be universal, but that does not show why Christian art is an example of didactic art.

Answer d – again the question takes words from the passage, 'worked hand in hand', and you may be tempted to think this to be the correct answer because of it.

Answer c – this is the correct answer because 'didactic' means 'intending to teach or to instruct'. Nowhere in the paragraph is the word 'teach' or 'instruct' used, but the third sentence is all about giving people a lesson.

key terms

didacticism

Instructing or teaching, generally in matters of morality.

■ Artists and history

Artists have a historical role. They have captured (i.e. portrayed in permanent form in that time) people, places and events that help us to visualize their life and times.

Behind some works of art the intention may have been to make a historical record, but so much of the world of art unintentionally provides an insight into times past. Portraits of famous people are interesting but portraits in general have served to show something of the dress and fashions as well as the poverty of people in the past. Paintings like those mentioned in paragraph 10 of the article on didactic art let us see something of the environment of those centuries.

The medieval *Bayeux Tapestry,* which is a lengthy embroidery, purposely records pictorially the historical events of the Norman Conquest of England up to and including 1066. It is a priceless work of art but the

Part of the Bayeux Tapestry

intention was to provide a historical record and to educate. This was part of the role of the embroiderers. Compare this with a much more modern work, that of Picasso in 1937.

In 1937, during the Spanish Civil War, the town of Guernica was mercilessly bombed. In his painting, *Guernica,* the Spanish artist, Picasso, does not seek to record the historical event – rather he uses it to express deeply felt horror of human violence and the suffering resulting from it. It has been described as revealing 'the dark side of life'. Is the work didactic? It is certainly significant and reaches into one's consciousness more than a report of the bombing. If it is not a historical record, it is a historical reminder. Sometimes, because of the *magnitude* of the horrors of war, famine and human disasters, we become almost immune, unable to feel the agony. Picasso's rage is personal, but the painting is universal and long lasting, continuing to convey through its images man's savage inhumanity to man. The painting is abstract and conveys a spirit of brokenness. Everything in it, beast and human, screams out.

Guernica, Picasso

89

analyse this

artists today, their role and their work

1 Artists have always had views about society and politics. Charlotte Bronte's novel, *Jane Eyre*, published in 1847 is the story of an independent-minded, educated young lady of limited means. The book conveys something of country life and the conventions of the different classes. It is a piece of creative fiction, but it does express in one paragraph, through the words of the character Jane, the author's views about gender roles.

Women are supposed to be very calm generally: but women feel just as men feel; they need exercise for their faculties, and a field for their efforts as much as their brothers do; they suffer from too rigid a restraint, too absolute a stagnation, precisely as men would suffer; and it is narrow-minded in their more privileged fellow-creatures to say that they ought to confine themselves to making puddings and knitting stockings, to playing on the piano and embroidering bags. It is thoughtless to condemn them for their sex.

2 Artists of all kinds may have strong views and their art becomes a vehicle for those views. For example, the writer George Orwell, in his book, *Animal Farm*, written in 1945, creates a fable that is a clear attack upon the totalitarian government of Soviet Russia. George Bernard Shaw's play, *Mrs. Warren's Profession*, written in 1893 is an attempt to show that society was to blame for prostitution because women were underpaid, undervalued and overworked. These are not works of overt propaganda. They have literary merit and are meant to be appreciated as such – yes and enjoyed – but the message comes through clearly. In the Spanish Civil War Picasso supported the Republicans against the Fascists and decreed that his painting *Guernica* should not be returned to Spain until the Fascists were vanquished.

3 The will to create. It is possible that artists nowadays do not see themselves as having a social role. They have the skills, the sensitivity, the imagination and the ability to create, and they are motivated to do so. This applies to all the arts, and although performers are expected to remain true to the original creation, the opera, the ballet the drama and the music, there is scope for them to be creative in the role – to use their artistic sensitivity and skill to great effect.

4 Modern art. In the past, society has *given* the artist a role by commanding religious works: paintings, sculpture, oratorios. Today the artist is still a product of society, aware of its customs and traditions, but she or he anticipates the future, and is ready to kick against society's conventions. Within her or his social framework the artist creates a personal role and the works she or he produces may sometimes seem very outlandish to the public at large, as some of the exhibits for the Turner Prize at the Tate Gallery at the end of the twentieth and beginning of the twenty-first century have shown.

5 Today society is less cohesive. It does not easily hang together so that we cannot clearly say what 'Britishness' is. There is no standard religion; instead there is a variety

of religions, but little religious observance. There are the more conventional artists, including those who do portraits to order or enjoy capturing a country scene. But it is the outlandish, the 'avant garde' (innovators or pioneers) – the products of this lack of cohesion and direction – whom we hear most about and who are subject to criticism. They are criticized by the traditionalists and/or by those who see no merit or artistic skill in modern works. Here is a list of some of the works of art submitted for the Turner Prize over the last few years:

- a pickled sheep;

- the artist's actual bedroom set out as it appeared one morning, complete with unmade bed, bed stains, cigarette ends, knickers lying around, a used condom and an empty vodka bottle;

- a light flicking on and off in an empty room;

- a written description of a pornographic movie;

- a ceiling covered with squares of coloured perspex;

- monolithic pillar;

- a film of Canary Wharf, London, shot from a moving crane.

6 These last four works were entered for the prize in 2002. They, and other submissions, collectively have been described by the Culture Minister, also an artist, as 'cold, mechanized, conceptual bullshit!' Forgive the word. He used it and it was reported in the press. *The Times* newspaper thought that The Turner Prize had been 'dominated by the played-out joke that is conceptual art.'

7 John Butler, who lives in the grounds of Newstead Abbey, where Byron lived, was interested in the local garden show where one of the events was for one vegetable and one flower. His idea was to place an onion with a sage flower and call the exhibit *Stuffing – Still Life, by Damonion Hirts*. Damien Hirst was the artist who assembled his rubbish to create a work of art. John's idea did not end up in the New Tate Gallery but it does indicate the kind of humorous reaction to some of the excesses of conceptual art.

8 Just because they receive so much publicity it is a mistake to think that the Turner Prize submissions represent the whole body of art in this country. The Turner Prize encourages what is daring and experimental and described as 'conceptual', but there are other opportunities for more traditional works. Modern art is about concepts – ideas and connections – and it challenges the viewer to respond in some way.

9 There may be many definitions of the word 'conceptual', but a concept is an abstract idea. Much of the conceptual art is three-dimensional, or produced by a video camera. Sometimes it is an arrangement of things, as is the case with Tracey Emin's bedroom.

10 This conceptual art is supported by those artists who believe that art has to be vibrant, and according to Rachel Campbell Johnston of *The Times* of 1 November 2002 it has 'to ask questions and breach popular boundaries'. This may provide a clue about what the role of the artist actually is. The artist has to experiment; to find new

and compelling ways of expressing thoughts about the modern world; the chaos it seems to be in and relating this to some of the traditional and universal concepts such as social order, justice and pity.

11 You may find it difficult to assign a role to any of the artists listed above. Their motivation may have been to win the money and achieve fame. Tracey Emin's work *Everyone I've Slept With 1963–1992* was bought for £40,000. It consists of a tent with 103 names embroidered on it. Many of the names are friends and family rather than lovers.

12 Countries have often thought of the arts as promoting a sense of unity and national belonging and where this is true it helps to define the role of the artist. But we are too early into this latest phase of conceptual art to determine if it has a Britishness about it.

13 What does seem to be true is that the artist follows his or her own inclinations and we judge the results according to the intellectual and emotional effects the works have upon us and the skill and artistry in the execution of the work. We expect our artists to create. We expect them to be innovative. What we can do is to study what is on offer and decide what is worthy. One of the problems of conceptual art is that we could all fancy our chances of having a go, but why won't my dustbin win a prize?

Questions

Here are some multiple-choice questions.

1 Which of the four alternatives, a, b, c or d, best describes Jane's view in the extract in point 1?

   a Women have little opportunity for physical exercise.

   b Women want to do all the things men do.

   c Women are less privileged than men.

   d Women should stick to domestic duties.

2 In point 3 the writer is really saying which of the following?

   a Artists have no social role.

   b They do not see themselves as having a role.

   c Those who perform the works of others, as does a singer or an actor, cannot be creative.

   d All performers should stick to the music, the choreography or the script.

3 According to paragraph 4:

  a Society gives the artist a role.

  b The artist does not relate to society in any way.

  c The artist conforms to social conventions.

  d The artist's role is personal rather than social.

4 According to point 5 the avant garde:

  a are traditional in their art;

  b enjoy capturing a country scene;

  c seek something new in their art;

  d are criticized by everyone.

5 John Butler's idea, described in point 7, is meant to be which of the following?

  a A piece of mockery.

  b A piece of irony.

  c A modern work of art.

  d a and b.

6 Which of the following ideas about conceptual art is/are not contained in this passage (points 9 and 10)?

  a It comes from abstract thought.

  b It is experimental.

  c It breaks popular conventions.

  d It is dying out.

7 From reading the last three points which of the following do you think is the 'best-fit' statement?

  a It is difficult to assign a role to any of the Turner Prize entries.

  b It will always be impossible to see our modern art as British.

  c The artist and the public both follow their own inclinations.

  d Dustbins do not win prizes.

analyse
this

Is the second case study, 'Artists today, their role and their work', a straightforward factual account or does the author show or imply any opinions? Write about 350 words expressing your point of view, using evidence and illustration from the passage. Your work should show clearly by your selections from the passage and your comments that you differentiate between fact and opinion.

8

Artists and interaction with their audiences:

public participation in the arts and the value of art education

A survey by the reputable Office of National Statistics for the Arts Council of England is a very useful start to this chapter because it begins with a statistical account of our attendance at arts events and raises the question of interaction between artist and audience. Interaction in a theatre is very different from that in a cinema. In the case of the theatre the audience can interact immediately with the actors. In the cinema the audience can *react* immediately to what happens on screen but there is no immediate *interaction* between screen actors and audience. There is a delay in the development of interaction, if any develops at all. This kind of interaction is referred to as *disjointed interaction*.

The artist may need a sense of audience, but where is the audience and how does the artist know what it thinks? How do composers and writers, as well as artists, receive any feedback, which is essential if any interaction is to develop?

There can be practical advantages in an arts education but the importance lies in the kinds of personal qualities that an arts education can help to develop – for example sensitivity and spirituality – but we should not forget that the arts are meant to be interesting and enjoyable.

■ The Arts Council survey

In 2002 the Arts Council of England published a lengthy report following a survey by the Office of National Statistics (ONS). The ONS chose a sample of people representative of the population and asked them to complete a questionnaire. The report entitled *Arts in England: Attendance, Participation and Attitudes in 2001*, attempts to show the level of interest and participation in the arts. According to a press release, the investigation showed that the vast majority of adults think that schoolchildren should be able to take part in the arts and that over three-quarters of adults had attended at least one arts event in the year before the survey. The press release also reported that '73% said that the arts play a valuable role in the life of the country and thought that arts from different cultures contribute a lot to this country' (joint press release from the Arts Council of England and Resource, 16 October 2002: www.resource.gov.uk/news/press_article).

analyse this

The following table, taken from the report, shows the level of attendance at a variety of events. It is quite straightforward to follow. Age groups are shown horizontally and the arts event vertically. At the bottom of each age column is the total number of people in the age group who were questioned. Look at the table. How many 16 to 24-year-olds attended a jazz concert? Work it out. The answer appears after the questions.

Percentage attending arts events, by age

Event Percentage	16–24	25–34	35–44	45–54	55–64	65–74	75+	All
Film	88	77	68	54	36	27	12	55
Play or drama	26	23	29	31	34	25	15	27
Musical	27	23	23	28	28	22	16	24
Carnival, street arts or circus	29	30	29	22	17	15	9	23
Art, photography or sculpture exhibition	17	18	20	22	23	19	10	19
Craft exhibition	7	14	17	20	25	21	13	17
Pantomime	8	13	19	12	12	13	11	13
Live dance event	17	14	10	13	14	10	6	12
Cultural festival	15	13	11	10	9	7	5	10
Classical music	4	6	8	12	16	14	12	10
Event connected with books or writing	7	9	9	9	8	6	4	8
Event including video or electronic art	12	12	7	6	3	2	–	7
Opera or operetta	4	4	4	7	8	9	6	6
Jazz concert	4	6	6	6	7	5	2	5
Base	**525**	**1025**	**1141**	**963**	**837**	**819**	**732**	**6042**

Questions

1 Make a note of any of these events that you have attended in the last year.

2 Write two or three paragraphs on why you think that a higher proportion of those questioned went to see a film than went to see a play. Any comment on how the percentages for film and play change as the age increases?

Answer to the problem

The jazz concert was attended by 4 per cent of the total number (525) questioned.

$$4 \div 100 \times 525 = 21$$

■ Why is film the most popular art form?

One of the reasons why film is the most popular of cultural events is that it is so dynamic. It can show so much more than any other type of performance apart from television. It can show you other countries and cities; it can present crowds; it can present impossible, spectacular happenings through special effects and generally create a world that appeals, but leaves little to, the imagination. Like the theatre it can draw strong reactions from the audience but, of course, the reactions have no effect upon the actors' performance in the film.

■ Stage plays

Stage musicals can have spectacular scene changes, as in *Les Miserables*, or exhilarating dancing, as in *Chicago*, but in comparison with film or television, stage plays are static and are restricted in the kinds of effects they can create. Stage productions show only three sides, the fourth side being where the audience is. What the theatre does provide is real people and the action is 'live', happening there and then, something that causes tension for the actors and an element of excitement for the audience. Stage acting involves not only interaction with other members of the cast but also a direct appeal to the audience. The performers have to project their voices to all parts of the theatre and they are able to respond to the audience's reaction.

key terms

interaction

This word means action and reciprocal or return action. There is interaction when person A asks person B a question and B replies.

■ Audience

With film and television, if there is no live audience there is no instant or spontaneous interaction between performers and audience, no two-way process. The film audience is watching what has already been done The performers are not in attendance. In the case of television there is no assembled audience. The members of the audience are scattered in their own homes and so there is no collective response as there can be from a cinema audience. The film audience reacts to what happens on film, but it makes no difference and has no effect at the time. Response to a film begins well after it is made – it comes from the critics and the audiences. This is a kind of disjointed interaction, a delay between action and reaction; as if Person B comes back a week later to respond to Person A's question. The delayed response, praising or criticizing individual performances and the production, is likely to have an effect upon future performances by individual actors and by production units. Popularity of the film as evidenced by the numbers who go to see it is a very important feedback. That is why we have had James Bond films for over 40 years.

It should not be forgotten that film stars have fans and fan clubs in which the interaction is by correspondence, generally asking for a signed photograph of one's favourite star.

With theatre there is spontaneous and immediate interaction. The actors perform. The audience gasps, sighs, shrieks, laughs, applauds, according to the performance, and the audience's response affects the actors. A positive response from the audience encourages the actors.

Other live performances before an audience, such as concerts and the ballet, compare with a play except that audience, reaction is restricted to the end of a performance, the end of an act or after a virtuoso performance, for example by a very talented performer.

In which of the events listed in the table above do you think there is the greatest interaction between actors and audience, in which the former positively try to get the audience to respond? Do you know the answer? Oh yes, you do! And what's more, when the pantomime is nearing the end someone always comes on stage to make the audience sing. In pantomimes even adults hiss, boo, cheer and sing, so the interaction is strong and immediate.

In rock and pop concerts there is a more lively kind of interaction between group and audience for the latter are apt to bounce and twist and jump up and down in unison and often the lead singer will appeal to the audience in a way similar to the pantomime artist.

But what about the static art event – the art exhibition? What possible kind of interaction can there be between artist and audience? In fact 'viewers' seems a more appropriate term than 'audience'! You do not normally find a whole crowd viewing a work of art and responding collectively. But remember from the previous chapter what Herbert Read said: 'The artist needs a sense of audience', which is not the same thing as 'audience'. Artists cannot present themselves before their works of art for every viewing. Like film and audience there is no spontaneous and immediate interaction between artist and audience. What the established poet, author, composer or artist knows is that out there is firstly a group of people who are interested in the particular art form – poetry, novels, music, painting or sculpture – and, secondly, there is a smaller group that is interested in his or her particular works. The composer receives his or her feedback through the medium of the band or orchestra at concerts.

Artists receive feedback on their creations in a variety of ways, for example:

- reviews of their works;

- interest shown by connoisseurs of art, music, literature (people recognized as experts);

- demand by the public, for example by purchase of publications or attendance at a gallery or musical performance;

- purchase of recordings.

In such ways artists get to know their 'audiences' and will be guided by them. This does not mean that they will produce more of the same to please the audience. On the contrary, having an appreciative audience or readership may encourage the artist to begin something quite revolutionary to startle his or her public and make it think. Artists may not meet the 'audience', but they need a 'sense' of it; they need to know that out there people admire their work. It is important for motivation.

analyse this

Write two or three paragraphs explaining the difference between a and either b *or* c, below:

a the interaction between a painter and his audience;

b the interaction between a television 'soap' production, such as *Eastenders* or *Coronation Street,* and its audience;

c the interaction between a rock or pop group and its audience.

(Chapter 10 has a section on 'soap' productions.)

analyse this

participation in the arts

Here is another table for you to examine. Just look through it and see if anything surprises you and make a note of it.

Percentage participating in arts activities, by age

Art form	Activity	16–24	25–34	35–44	45–54 Percentage	55–64	65–74	75+	All
Literature	Read for pleasure	69	75	73	76	75	75	66	73
	Buy a novel, fiction, play or poetry for yourself	45	53	50	57	53	43	34	49
	Write any stories or plays	6	4	3	2	4	2	2	3
	Write any poetry	6	4	4	3	4	3	1	3
Dance	Clubbing	69	53	25	9	4	3	2	25
	Do any other dance (but not fitness class)	7	6	6	10	10	9	7	8
	Do any ballet	1	1	1	*	*	*	*	1
Music	Play a musical instrument (for own pleasure)	20	10	9	7	6	7	4	9
	Sing to an audience (or rehearse)	6	3	3	4	5	4	3	4
	Play a musical instrument (or rehearse)	7	2	2	3	3	2	1	3
	Write or compose a piece music	6	2	1	1	•	1	•	2
Drama	Perform in a play or drama (or rehearse)	8	1	2	2	2	1	1	2
Visual arts	Painting, drawing, print making or sculpture	30	18	13	11	12	8	6	14
	Photography as an artistic activity	8	5	5	8	8	6	4	6
	Buy any original works of art	2	6	8	10	7	5	2	6
	Make any films or videos as an artistic activity	4	1	1	1	2	1	•	2
Crafts	Textile crafts such as embroidery, sewing, etc.	10	11	11	14	20	18	14	14
	Buy any original handmade crafts	10	13	15	17	14	7	5	12
	Wood crafts	8	4	5	6	6	5	4	6
	Other crafts such as calligraphy, pottery or jewellery making	3	5	4	4	4	3	3	4
Other	Create original artworks or animation using computer	8	6	5	3	3	1	1	4
	Help with running of an arts/cultural event or arts organisation	3	2	3	5	4	3	2	4
Base		**525**	**1025**	**1141**	**963**	**837**	**819**	**732**	**6042**

This table is about participation in the arts: being actively involved by acting in a play, for example, or playing your trumpet at a school or college concert. Of all the people who buy tapes and CDs to listen to music I wonder how many have actually played a musical instrument or sung in public, including karaoke.

What seems surprising about the table of participation in the arts is that it includes clubbing! Do you think of clubbing as one of the arts, a performing art? It is an activity, certainly, but is it an art form? The Arts Council thinks so, although when you look at the rest of the activities you will see that they mostly involve some skill, some artistry and some confidence. (Look! According to the table, 2 per cent of the 75-year-olds and over go clubbing! I'd like to see them.)

However much or however little skill and artistry clubbing may demand of the participants, Broughton and Brewster, in their book entitled *How to DJ Properly*, published by Bantam Press in 2002, believe that disc jockeying is an art and a science of playing records. Their book on that subject runs to nearly 300 pages. It includes such topics as:

- beatmatching;
- stops and spinbacks;
- mixing mp3s;
- EQ;
- hot-mix;
- how to mix harmonically;
- how to beat-juggle;
- how to sample without going to jail;
- how to be famous; and
- how to be great.

The book is quite technical in nature. It has a helpful glossary at the end, which provides some useful theory, and the section on how to make a track should appeal to any adventurous DJ. As well as the science of DJ-ing, there are some down-to-earth quotes, expressing, it seems, the art of the business – if you can stand some of the language used. Here is an example, without that language:

When I make a
tune I have the
beats for my feet,
I have the strings
for my head, I
have the vocals
for my heart and I
have the bass for
my groin

(DJ Rap DJ Times)

'We're all artistes now!'

Question

Either a) pick out a few interesting facts and figures from the table and write two or three paragraphs about them, or b) write a comment (two or three paragraphs) on this table, showing whether or not it is useful and interesting.

analyse
this

'performing', by Vanessa Young

Look at this article by a 16-year-old girl.

I want to talk about the role of the performers because acting, singing and dancing are my greatest loves – outside my family, of course. I got my break as a five-year-old in Wizard of Oz. *Audiences didn't worry me. I loved the stage and quickly took up dancing lessons of all kinds.*

After that I appeared regularly at my local theatre in quite a few presentations and every Christmas I was a dancer in the professional pantomime for about six weeks. Performance is the thing, but you strive for perfection and so have to work and rehearse hard. I find it interesting studying the cast and the peculiarities of some of the individuals; the show-offs and those who try to upstage their fellow actors. You even get cases of an actor missing out his or her lines and then looking around at someone as if to imply that this other person is to blame. It is a cut-throat profession, but it is full of helpful people. I've done some filming as an extra. It can be exciting when you are performing, but there is often a lot of waiting about whilst the director changes his mind and the crew move the lighting and the cameras.

As they say, there's no business like show business.

The writer of that article clearly enjoys acting in spite of, or perhaps because of, some of the difficulties. She has learned something about the attitudes of other people and has come to accept hard work and regular rehearsal. This learning is of benefit in all walks of life for it is almost always better to be able to do something yourself rather than to watch other people do it. It applies to all the performing arts: singing, dancing, acting, yes, and karaoke, if you like, but sometimes, when it means performing in public, it does take some confidence. There are hundreds of things we cannot do, but each one of us can take on something and come to enjoy the satisfaction of doing it. You could try your hand at some conceptual art – something for your bedroom, perhaps.

Using the case study as an example write about one of the artistic activities in which you participate – perhaps one of the activities mentioned in the table showing participation in the arts. In particular, explain what you enjoy about participating and how it benefits you. As an alternative you may write your views on the inclusion of clubbing in the list of arts activities. Make your views clear, but give reasons for and against.

■ The place and value of arts in education

Successive governments have thought the arts important enough to have them on the National Curriculum so that they are compulsory subjects in state schools from the beginning of schooling up to the end of year 9, when they are available but optional. Music and art are common in all state schools but not all schools offer performing arts, such as drama or dance.

Some schools offer the opportunity to learn a musical instrument, to sing or perform at a concert, to be a member of a choir or to take part in a play. These opportunities are offered because they are thought by schools to be an important part of one's education.

Some children have private lessons to learn to play an instrument or lessons in dance, theatre and singing. They may also belong to groups such as choirs and amateur drama and dance groups.

analyse this

Discuss, in small groups, the value of art education at your school including:

- skills learned;
- experience of working with different materials;

- experience, sensitivity and appreciation acquired;

- what you have acquired that you would not have acquired without art education;

- whether what you learned helped in other ways;

- whether you have extended your interest outside school.

(Remember, the discussion is about the subject, art, not about personalities.)

analyse this

Here is an extract from *The Story of Art* by E.H. Gombrich:

Art teaching seems to me to be the sixth element and a very important one in the contemporary situation. It was in the teaching of art to children that the revolution in modern education made itself first felt. At the beginning of this century art teachers began to discover how much more they could get out of children if they abandoned the soul-destroying drill of traditional methods. It was the time, of course, when these methods had anyhow become suspect through the success of Impressionism and the experiments of Art Nouveau. The pioneers of this movement of liberation . . . in Vienna wanted the children's talent to unfold in freedom till they were ready for the appreciation of artistic standards.

The results . . . achieved were so spectacular that the originality and charm of children's work became the envy of trained artists. In addition, psychologists came to value the sheer pleasure which children experienced in messing about with paint and plasticine. It was in the art class that the ideal of 'self-expression' was first appreciated by large numbers. Today we use the term 'child-art' as a matter of course without even realizing that it contradicts all the notions of art held by previous generations. Most members of the public have been conditioned by this education, which has taught them a new tolerance.

Questions

1 Which one of the following points does the author make?

a In the present time it is very important for art to be taught.

b Art teaching has always been important.

c As things were at the time of writing, the author thought that art teaching was very important.

d It is very important to teach contemporary art.

2 Which of the following alternatives best explains the meaning of the phrase 'soul-destroying drill of traditional methods'?

a   Repetitive teaching is boring and turns students off.

b   Teaching art according to a fixed routine destroys any spark of enthusiasm students have for the subject.

c   The routine teaching of art, common in the past, kills off any feeling for art that the students have.

d   The drill of traditional methods destroyed the soul.

3 Which of the following is the best description of what the author is saying?

a   The pioneers of liberation in art wanted children to have complete freedom in their art work.

b   The emphasis was upon teaching children to appreciate artistic standards.

c   The pioneers of liberation in art believed that giving children freedom in art would prepare them for the appreciation of artistic standards.

d   They wanted children to develop their talent in freedom until they were able to appreciate standards in art.

4 What was the effect of children's art on other people?

a   Established artists envied the originality and charm of children's work.

b   Established artists valued the pleasure that children experienced.

c   Psychologists envied the sheer pleasure that children experienced.

d   Established artists envied the originality and charm of children's work and the psychologists valued the sheer pleasure that children experienced.

key terms

art nouvea

New art, or new style. It was a European and American movement beginning at the end of the nineteenth century. It was a feature seen, for example, in interior design and wrought-iron work.

impressionism

A very important and influential art movement started in France in the latter half of the nineteenth century. The Impressionist exhibition in Paris in 1874 included works by Monet, Renoir and other important French artists. You really need to look at some examples of Impressionism. ▶

> The aim of this school was to depict real, natural life, 'straight from nature' and to capture the effect of changing light. Typical of the technique was the way in which bright colours were almost flicked onto the canvas. Impressionism was very different from the traditional, more formal, highly finished works and its absence of outline tended to create an overall effect upon one's feelings .

analyse
this
why learn about it?

Think of all the subjects you have studied:

- mathematics;
- English;
- science;
- history;
- geography,

and so on. Perhaps you did not enjoy some of these subjects. It is also possible that a few students would say that only basic mathematics and English, possibly ICT, will be of any use to them in their lives and would wonder why they should study anything else. They will be able to check their change, read, write, use a word processor and talk to other people. However, what will they talk about? Their lives would seem rather limited. I would rather hear a conversation – even a heated discussion – between two people who understand what they are talking about than one where they argue in ignorance. The point about education is that its purpose is to introduce everyone to the main branches of learning; to give a *wide* education that stresses experience, skill and understanding and encourages thought and evaluation. This wide-ranging education helps to prepare people for their future lives as social beings; its purpose is not to train them for jobs, although they will be more acceptable to an employer than a maths-English-ICT-only applicant.

If you agree with these general principles – and you probably would not be doing general studies if you did not agree – then you will understand that each subject makes a contribution to the education and social development of students, and not only students.

So what does arts education do for people? We have already considered the value of performing arts. In the first place, education in all the arts can provide an interest and enjoyment for a lifetime. It helps you to view or listen or read with a greater understanding and therefore greater interest and there is much satisfaction in being able to use your knowledge to help you to appreciate fully something new.

You can consider all kinds of practical reasons why such education can be of benefit to you – for example, it can lead to an interest or a hobby. But, like history, a study of the arts puts us in touch with the present human situation as well as connecting us with the past. This past is a wealthy heritage, which we can examine for its beauty, its skill and artistry, its didacticism and for its record of history and historical development.

However, the essential value and benefit of an education in the arts is the way it can encourage and develop inner qualities. The arts are food for thought and feelings, sensitivity, spirituality. They can arouse emotions from ecstasy to quiet solemnity; from humour to misery; from sensuality to spirituality. And in the end we evaluate them according to our own experience.

We must not make too much of this spirituality, for different people are affected differently by the arts. If you visit the New Tate Gallery in London you will be tempted to laugh at some of the exhibits. And why not? But do it quietly, for someone will be taking the painting or sculpture seriously, as you will be doing as you come across something that captures your interest or imagination. Remember, the arts are meant to be enjoyed and the more experience and understanding you gain the more you will enjoy them.

◼ Pop art

If you have never taken much interest in painting you may be surprised to discover pop art. The following picture is an example of the work of the American artist, Andy Warhol (1928–87).

Marilyn, Andy Warhol

Pop art was inspired by the commercial world; by consumerism and advertising. Some of the paintings, especially those by Roy Lichtenstein, are like comic strips. This 'brand' of art is a reminder that artists can be inspired, or at least motivated, by whatever is around them. Warhol even painted tins of Campbell's soup. Pop art is often recognizable, captivating and frequently funny.

9

Art and music:
artistic movements and the appreciation of different styles of music

This chapter offers a broad understanding and an appreciation of the major artistic movements and different styles of music. It includes illustrations of selected paintings, sculpture and architecture. It presents 16 coloured plates showing works of art ranging from 400 BCE to the late twentieth century, and then asks you to study an art timeline that gives three pieces of information:

● dates of particular periods or schools of art;

● some examples from each of the periods; and

● the names of the artists.

To explain the basic principles of each period of art this is followed by a glossary. Do not bother to read it, unless you cannot help it – *use* it as you need it.

When you have come this far you will be ready for an activity that asks you to study a few pictures of works of art and place them in their correct school or period. If you have any doubts go over the timeline again and read the section that follows the activity, entitled 'aesthetic evaluation', which explains that approval of a work of art does not mean that it is beautiful. Works like Hieronymus Bosch's hell scenes are highly rated! If you like the music of Marilyn Manson and wear any of his iconic gear you will understand this business of rating the hideous highly.

The last section of the chapter ranges over many different types of music, pointing out the different conventions for various types of musical performance and how performer image is important in the pop world but of little significance in the world of classical music.

■ See for yourselves

You will already know the names of a number of artists and may have seen either their works or reproductions of their works and photographs of them in art books. In most towns there are moderately priced bookshops offering books about famous artists at reasonable prices.

In this chapter we hope to show something of the range of art over the centuries and the different artistic movements. The eight pages of colour prints begin with the Parthenon at Athens, built about 450 BCE, and end with the Sydney Opera House, built in 1973.

Before you do any serious reading, look at the 16 colour plates of works of art. Notice some of the differences in style, from the earliest through to the latest, and make a note of any that you find interesting, attractive, appealing or fascinating in any way.

analyse this

1   Which word do you think best describes the *Mona Lisa* by Leonardo da Vinci?

   a   cheerful;

   b   puzzled;

   c   distressed;

   d   thoughtful.

2   In a few sentences briefly describe the *Kitchenmaid* in the Vermeer painting.

3   Describe in one sentence the mood of the painting by Renoir, *Moulin de la Galette.*

4   Pick out any religious paintings.

5   Look at Piet Mondrian's painting. Broadway is a great street in New York City, famous for its theatres. Boogie woogie is a kind of blues or jazz music for the piano in which the left hand plays a persistent and repeated bass rhythm while the right hand plays the melody. It is generally fast. Now try to explain in five sentences what Mondrian's painting is all about. How is the title related to the painting?

6   The Salvador Dali work is a sculpture. Give your reasons in a few sentences to show why the watch is melting. The sculpture is a piece of surrealism – a fantasy, an expression of the subconscious mind, or a dream.

7   Describe in a few sentences what you think are the differences in style and brushwork between Van Gogh's *Bedroom at Arles* and Turner's *The Fighting Téméraire.*

■ Introduction to the art timeline

You will have noticed that the illustrations in the 16 coloured plates are in time order. The following timeline is a guide to the timing of the beginnings of new schools or styles of art that were innovative (brought in changes and new ideas) in any or all of the following features:

● subject;

● style;

● treatment;

● technique;

● materials.

Before you start the timeline have a look at the picture of Chiswick House. It was built in about 1729. Its architects were influenced by the High Renaissance architect, Andrea Palladio (1508–80).

Chiswick House, London

He had been influenced by his studies of the ruins of Roman classical antiquity and his buildings and his books on architectural design were regarded as the height of taste and fashion in eighteenth-century England. This villa (large country house with an estate), following Palladio's designs, was built along classical lines with a stately portico (colonnade, or roof supported by columns) and a rotunda (a round design with a dome). This example is given to show that despite the divisions of history's art into movements, schools or periods they are not completely 'watertight'. Styles cross these artificial 'boundaries'. Fashions can come and go. See also the Pre-Raphaelites in the glossary.

This timeline may seem long and complicated, but you do not have to memorize it – just use it for reference. At the end of the timeline there is a glossary explaining some of the terms used. To keep it under control, some periods in art development have been left out.

Date	Movement, School or Type of Art	Example of Type
400 BCE	Classical	Greek. Parthenon, Athens
300 BCE	art of Ancient	
200 BCE	Rome and Greece	Greek. Statue of Aphrodite/Venus de Milo
Common Era (Anno Domini)		
100	Rome	Roman. The Pantheon
500	Medieval	Religious works
1100	Norman architecture	Durham Cathedral. Rounded arches, doorways and windows Bayeux Tapestry
1200	Gothic architecture	Salisbury Cathedral. Pointed arches, doorways and windows
	Late Medieval	The Wilton Diptych
1300	Early Renaissance	Giotto – Kiss of Judas
	Moorish	Al Hambra, Islamic Palace
1400		Da Vinci – Mona Lisa
1500	Late of High Renaissance	Michelangelo – Frescoes of Sistine Chapel Titian – Mater Dolorsa
1600	Baroque	Caravaggio – Supper at Emmaus
	Flemish Baroque	Rembrandt – Self-portrait – in old age Vermeer – Kitchenmaid
	Indo-islamic	Taj Mahal

1700	Rococo (Palladian)	Fragonard – Girl on a Swing Chiswick House, London
1800	Romanticism	Gainsborough – Mr. and Mrs. Andrews Constable – Haywain Turner – The Fighting Téméraire
	Pre-Raphaelites	Rossetti – The Day Dream
	Impressionism	Pissarro – Place du Théâtre-Français, Spring Renoir – Moulin de la Galette Monet – Waterlilies
	Post Impressionism	Rodin – The Kiss Van Gogh – Bedroom at Arles
	Art nouveau	Style of architecture and interior decoration
1900	Expressionism	Munch – The Scream
	Cubism	Picasso – Violin and Grapes Guernica
	Abstract	Piet Mondrian – Broadway Boogie Woogie
1924	Surrealism	Dali – The Profile of Time Magritte – The Empire of Light
1950	Pop Art	Warhol – Four Campbell's Soup Cans
	Action Painting	Pollock – One (Number 31, 1950)
	Expressionist	Sydney Opera House
	Modern	London Dome
	Conceptual Art	Tracy Emin – The Tent The Bedroom

■ Glossary of terms used in the art timeline

Do not read this glossary. Use it like a dictionary, but note that it is not in alphabetical order – it is in order of appearance of the terms in the art timeline.

Parthenon – an ancient Greek temple dedicated to Athena (Goddess of Athens).

Medieval – in the style of the Middle Ages, i.e. from 400 to 1400 CE (AD).

Norman architecture – 1066 to 1150 CE. This refers to the buildings erected after Normans invaded this country in 1066, the main features of which are the rounded arches, like an upside-down letter U, and square towers. St John's chapel in the Tower of London is a well-preserved example of Norman architecture.

Gothic architecture – 1150–1500. This was a style that included pointed arches and the period is characterized by the building of great cathedrals with tall spires. The pointed arch was one of the reasons why cathedrals and churches could be built much higher.

Moorish – of the Moors, Muslims living in north-west Africa. They ruled Spain from the eighth to the seventeenth century.

Renaissance (rebirth) – a period from the 1300s to 1500s when a greater emphasis was placed on 'man'. Faces and bodies in art became more life-like. More emphasis was given to human beings and their place in the world. Look at the *Mona Lisa* and compare it with the faces in the Wilton Diptych.

Baroque – 1600s to 1700s – a difficult style to pin down because whilst it is concerned with balance and symmetry and interplay between light and dark (see the *Woman Taken in Adultery*) it can be very dramatic, rich in colour and urgently appeal to the emotions of the viewer. Baroque music is ornate and extravagant but has a definite form. Listen again to Vivaldi's *The Four Seasons.*

Indo-Islamic – built in Agra, India by the Moguls, a Muslim dynasty in 1648.

Rococo – a style of lightness, elegance, ornament and decoration, which appeared in France about 1700. Mainly a style for interior decoration with pastel colour. Paintings exhibit prettiness and gaiety.

Palladian – in the style of Andrea Palladio (1518–80), a Renaissance architect who designed palaces and churches using the classical forms of Rome, with an emphasis on symmetry and proportion.

Romanticism – a style that made imagination and emotion more important than intellectual discipline. Turner's painting of the *Fighting Téméraire* being towed away by a steam tug for breaking up as the last rays of the sun settle on the water would have aroused the emotions of the viewers in the late 1830s. Romantic music, beginning with Beethoven's, is more personal, more poetic than Baroque and it was more free to break through the traditional forms.

Pre-Raphaelites – a group of British painters formed in 1848 to work in the style of the early Italian Renaissance painters. The subjects of their paintings were literary, moral and religious. Their works were characterized by very fine detail.

Impressionism – see Chapter 8.

Post-impressionism – a reaction to impressionism that emphasized form and colour and gave more importance to the subject. Notice these features, strongly displayed in Van Gogh's *Bedroom at Arles*.

Art Nouveau – see Chapter 8.

Expressionism – a personal and intensely passionate and forceful style. Expressiveness is often achieved by exaggeration and distortion. See Munch's *The Scream*.

Cubism – a style developed by Braque and Picasso in France at the beginning of the twentieth century. It consists of geometrical shapes and tries to reveal something from different angles at the same time. It is concerned with structure and often shows different surfaces of the subject superimposed.

Abstract – a type of painting that presents forms and colours. The Mondrian *Broadway Boogie Woogie* is restricted to straight lines and only a few colours.

Surrealism – is an expression of conscious and unconscious experience. Often nightmarish, it is a rejection of reason and is a fascinating fantasy. See Dali's melting watch.

Pop art – see Chapter 8.

Action painting – achieved by splashing, dribbling or pouring paint onto a canvas, the artist relying upon the unconscious to produce a work of art. Jackson Pollock (1912–56) is supposed to have poured paint onto a canvas on the floor and ridden his bicycle through it. There is something appealing about some of his haphazard patterns in paint.

Expressionist modern – for example the Sydney Opera House. This modern, distinctive building harks back to expressionism – and its intensely passionate and forceful style. It sits there out in the harbour looking as if the wind is in its 'sails'.

Conceptual art – begins with the concept, the abstract idea which seems more important than the result of it. The concept may be presented in a variety of ways using a whole range of materials and artefacts – anything to hand, such as film, video, slide projector, photographs, garden utensils. Sometimes the objects are together as a unit, for example in Tracey Emin's 'bedroom'. Or the artist may assemble a collection of totally unrelated objects. A light switching itself on and off in an empty room won the Turner Prize in 2001.

analyse
this

Below are six black-and-white reproductions of works of art. Using the art timeline, or anything else that helps, see if you can place them within their school, type or movement. Extra points if you can also name the work of art and the artist.

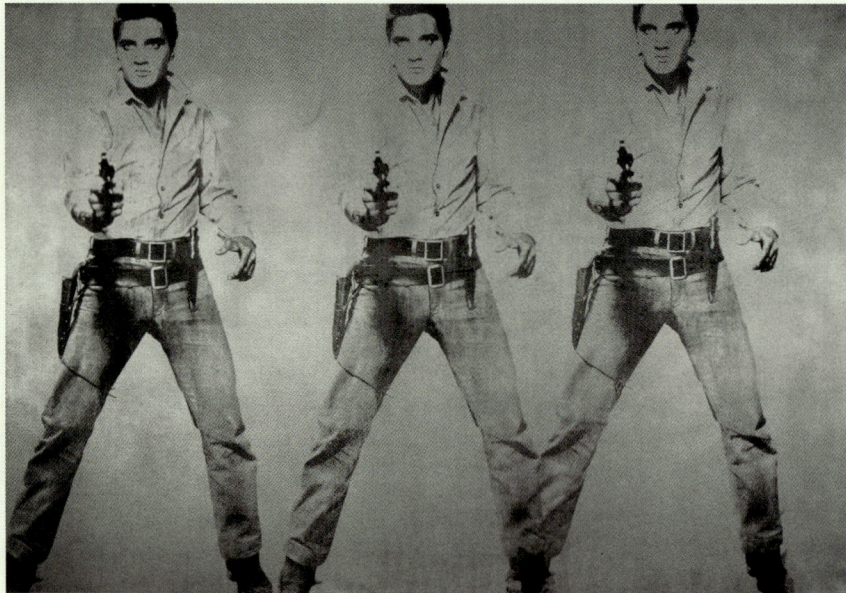

The Parthenon, Athens

The Wilton Diptych

The Mono Lisa, Leonardo da Vinci

The Sistine Chapel, Michaelangelo (detail, The Creation of Adam)

Mater Dolorosa, Titian

Woman Taken in Adultery, Rembrandt

The Kitchen Maid, Vermeer

The Taj Mahal

The Fighting Téméraire, Turner

Place du Théâtre Français, Pissarro

Le Moulin de la Galette, Renoir

Bedroom at Arles, Vincent van Gogh

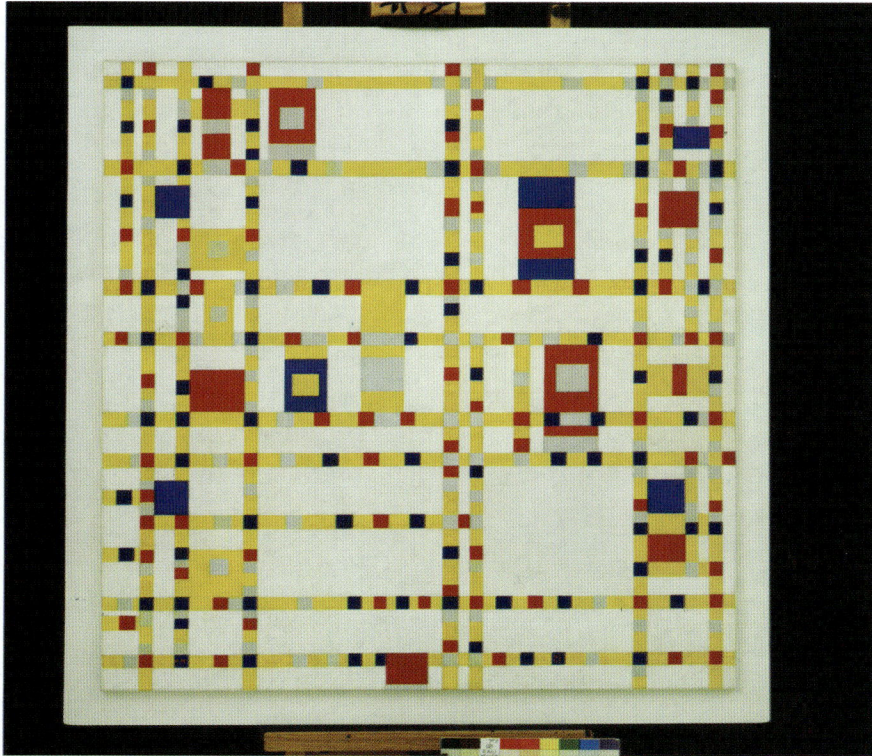

Broadway Boogie Woogie, Piet Mondrian

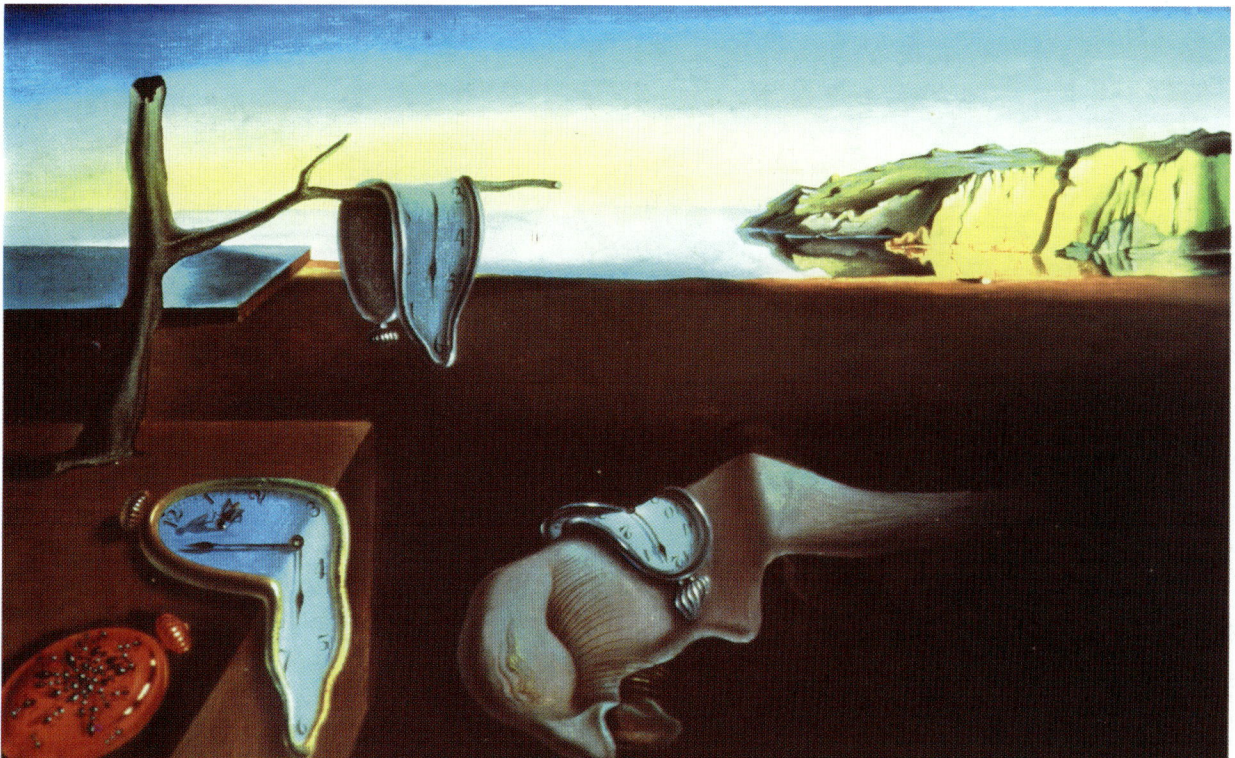

Profile of Time, Salvador Dali

Cans of Campbell's Soup, Andy Warhol

Sydney Opera House

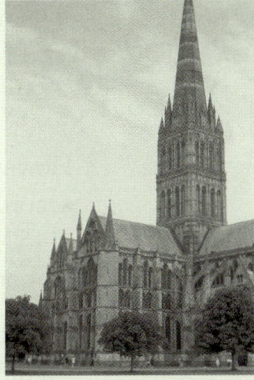

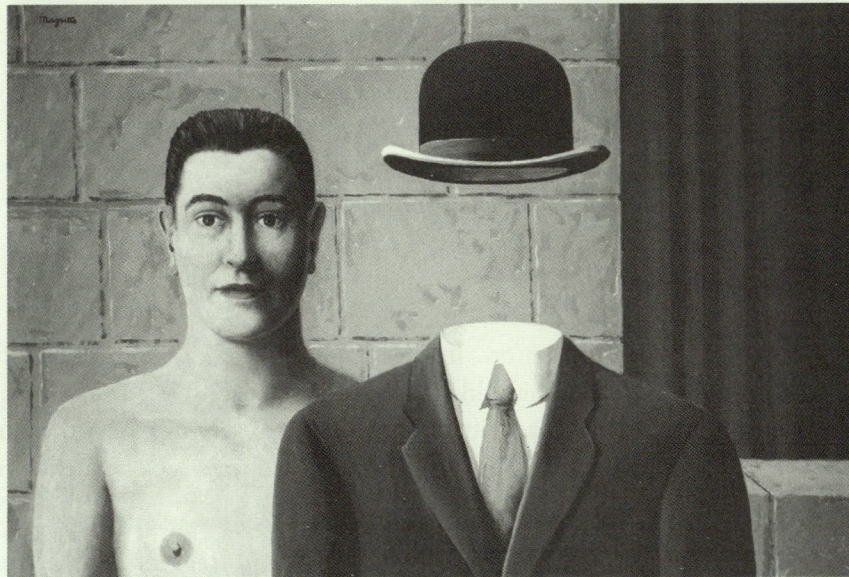

■ Aesthetic evaluation

By now, even if you have never made a study of art, you will have some experience of famous works and how they fit into the time scale and the periods. You will have formulated an opinion about some of them, in other words you will have made a personal evaluation. You may want to call it an aesthetic evaluation after you understand the meaning of 'aesthetic' (pronounced *eesthetic*). Aesthetic evaluation can mean these things:

- an appreciation of beauty;

- a sensitivity to beauty;

- an understanding of what it is that makes a painting, a poem a piece of music good;

- evaluation purely on beauty, not on any moral or social purpose.

However, do you think you can judge Dali's work *The Profile of Time* according to its beauty? Some of the paintings of Hieronymus Bosch (1450–1516) depict hideous fantasy figures of sinners in hell. Beautiful? Not at all!

In fact, we extend the meaning of the word *beauty* through the word 'aesthetic' to include such ideas as:

- awe;

- wonderment;

- grandeur;

- excitement;

- fascination;

- pity.

And so on. It may seem contradictory, but you often hear people say something like: 'I love this music; it is so sad!' Surprisingly, the second movement of Beethoven's Third Symphony, the funeral march, can be chillingly exciting. We do not always seek beauty, harmony, sweetness and light for our enjoyment.

Wilfred Owen, a poet writing in the First World War, described the horrors of that war: the trenches, the mud, the gas attacks and the ugly death. Why are the poems so appreciated? Because, as Owen himself said, the poetry is in the pity.

We may value a work of art because it introduces a new and exciting style. We may also value it because of the concept that prompted the work and the way in which it reveals or suggests that concept. Tracey Emin's bedroom is not beautiful in the accepted sense of the word. It conveys starkly a sense of degradation and depression, a rough awakening after a night of abandonment. However, we may find this work intensely interesting, if the owner ever puts it on display, because we identify with the mood, or because we come to appreciate something about the human condition that we pity. The best of the arts more than increase our understanding; they sharpen our imagination and refine our emotions. Picasso's *Guernica* encapsulates the horror undiluted and it is capable of affecting the viewer more than a press report of damage and hundreds of casualties caused by the bombing.

The painting of the *Mona Lisa* by Leonardo da Vinci (1452–1519) is very different and from a different age. This is beautiful in the traditional sense of the word. This unknown lady has a beautiful face and a warm round body but, more than that, her composure and facial expression suggest that she has a secret. Generations have argued over whether or not she is smiling. Interpret it as you will. She is often described as 'enigmatic' or puzzling. This is an example of beauty captured: it is art for art's sake. However, da Vinci was more than a painter of beautiful women. His cartoon (design for a painting) of *The Virgin and Child with St Anne* is a wonderful study of mystery and tenderness.

As well as fine religious settings, da Vinci was interested in what we now call physics and engineering. He produced designs for a giant catapult, a water wheel, an excavating machine and a flying machine (it would never have left the ground). Still, life for him was full of possibilities, of problems to solve. He was an innovator and a creator with a great thirst for knowledge. A Renaissance man!

Jean-Clarence Lambert in his introduction to *The Renaissance I* (1968) makes this essential point about the Renaissance. He refers to: 'painting, which at last restored to our eyes the treasure lost from sight with the gods of Greece and Rome and held in anathema by popes and doctors of the Holy Church – the human body!'

The sudden reappearance of the body typifies the new approach to the problem of man's attitude to the world as well as the world's attitude to man. Islamic art does not show the human body. Its art is highly patterned.

Giotto (1276–1337) is generally considered to be the founder of modern painting, for his figures are more lifelike than the flat figures of earlier artists. By the time we get to Titian (1487–1576) we arrive at a rich collection of portraits, religious scenes and figures from classical mythology, in which the people are real and modern with vibrant faces, showing character and emotion. His female figures have fine faces and his well-proportioned nudes are rather languidly erotic. In our collection of reproductions, Titian's *Mater Dolorosa* (1555), depicting the grieving Mother of Christ, shows a beautiful and fresh-faced Mary, young and virginal.

Such pictures were commissioned as religious images, but the artist moves away from the traditional representation of Mary by giving her an attractive quality which is not quite holy.

Now you have some idea of what aesthetic evaluation is. Is it something for the experts? Or can you join in?

analyse this

In making any kind of judgement or evaluation about art should we be guided by the critics or by experts who produce books on art? Or should we look for ourselves, ignore the experts and then make our own minds up? Write about 250 words on this controversial topic, dealing with both sides of the argument, and come to some conclusion.

analyse this

music appreciation

1   Some of the periods of art apply to the periods of music. So we speak of:

- Baroque music – the rich style of the seventeenth and early eighteenth centuries.

- Classical music – 1750–1830, tends to stick to basic conventional forms rather than express emotion. It is orderly and balanced, not given to extremes. There is nothing like the passion of Beethoven. Emotion is there, witness Handel's *Messiah* and some of the second movements of Mozart's piano concertos, but it is generally within a formal framework. (Note that the term 'classical' is also used in a general way to distinguish 'serious music' from light or popular music.)

- Romantic music – dating from about 1820, tends to be poetic, and very expressive, as much opera of the mid-eighteenth to the late-nineteenth century is.

2   Modern music, dating from the beginning of the twentieth century, is often experimental and innovative. The century gave us, to name but a few examples:

- jazz;

- swing;

- jive;

- boogie woogie;

- bebop;

- rock and roll;

- rhythm and blues;

- easy listening.

3   In the early part of the twenty-first century there is a wide variety of popular styles, examples of which may be heard on that up-to-date, eclectic (including all styles) programme *Top of the Pops*. Sky channels have different music programmes, some devoted to a particular type of music, others providing a variety of music. Looking up from writing this, I can switch to any of the following music channels on Sky and get a surrealistic video to accompany the music:

- P. Rock (Punk);

- MTV;

- VHI;

- Kiss;

- Smash Hits;

- Kerrang;

- Q;

- Magic;

- Base MTV Dance.

There are also programmes of classical music.

4   The way to listen to music – and custom has set the way – depends on the type of music, where one listens to it, and whether one is at home or at a concert. We do not have to learn how. We just follow what others do. Here you may like to look back at the section on pop and high culture in Chapter 6, where some of the ways of appreciating different types of music are described. Here is a brief summary:

- Classical concert – silence during the performance, applause at the end. It may be rapturous applause with shouts of 'encore' which is French for 'again' or 'let's have more of it'.

- Opera – much the same, although laughter is permitted where the plot is humorous, as is enthusiastic appreciation for a fine virtuoso, i.e. solo performance.

- Ballet – as for opera.

- Pop and rock concerts – in a field or in a concert hall, you cheer, wave, dance, jump and generally get as emotionally involved as you possibly can.

- Pop, rock on video or television – you watch the essential video whilst moving rhythmically but not too wildly.

- Clubbing – keep moving to the music in any way that is allowed.

- Pop on CD, tape or radio - you listen and bob about if you want to. One of the advantages of music relayed this way is that you can do other things – switch on, stick the earphones in and do your paper round, cycle to college, carry on a conversation, or most things.

There is nothing wrong with any of this as long as it's safe. Ideally people would be receptive to a wide range of music from early church music to rap, hip-hop and all contemporary pop.

5   For classical music, symphonies, small ensembles and opera there are ways and standards for judging music and the more one knows about the technical aspects the more one is able to evaluate a performance. For example, in an orchestral concert, is the music performed at the right tempo? Is there a proper blend of sound made up by the different instruments? Does the conductor have control over the orchestra and is he able to make it play with appropriate feeling? Sometimes concert goers take along the musical scores of the pieces of music on the programme. Much the same is expected for the opera, but we also expect the cast to sing well, in unison and solo – no flat notes or squeaks. We expect them to act well, with their voices, their expressions, their movement and gestures.

6   As you can see, although technical know-how increases one's enjoyment of such music one can still be moved by and enjoy the music without such knowledge. Some music is enjoyed straight away, because of its beauty or because it arouses some emotion, but other music may demand patient and intelligent listening before one comes to appreciate it.

7   In a general way, much of what has been said about classical music can apply to popular music. You expect the musicians to play well and you expect the singers to sing well, but the conventions are different. With some styles of music, such as rock and grunge, noises that are not pure notes and sounds produced by using the tremolo arm on a guitar to obtain a rapid alternation between different notes are part of the music idiom (character or form of expression). These sounds are rebellious and anarchistic (breaking the rules) and are often very exciting. Extreme groups have taken to smashing up their instruments, and that can probably be exciting, too, as long as it is safe.

8   Much more than classical music, pop music has to carry performer image. Groups have to be 'plugged' – sold to the public – and there must be many a good group that still waits for recognition and success because it has not had the publicity. Pop stars are subjected to the prying eyes of the hounds of the media. Whatever they do appears in the newspapers, especially if it's trouble.

9   A well-known British star, Robbie Williams, has recently signed a contract that could earn him £80 million, depending upon whether he successfully breaks into the US market. If he is not successful he will still do rather well. He has a good voice and to the amusement of his home audience he likes to clown around a bit during his performances. A typical reaction from America, where he needs to succeed, is 'why does he act so goofy?' This kind of criticism could spoil his chances. Image is everything.

Some of our classical conductors show a sense of humour, especially during the Last Night of the Proms, but it never seems to affect their careers.

Questions

Here are some questions about the above text.

1 According to point 1, Romantic music is which of the following?

a Rich in style.

b Controlled in expression.

c Jazz.

d Very expressive.

2 The word 'eclectic' is used in point 3. Which of the following comes nearest to its meaning?

a Up to date.

b Stylish.

c Selected from different types.

d Modern.

3 Also in point 3, videos accompanying pop music are described as 'surrealistic'. This means which one of the following?

a The videos are synchronised with the music.

b The videos are unreal.

c The videos are a fantasy.

d The videos match the style of music.

4 Point 4. The way we listen to music is determined by which of the following?

a It is governed by rules.

b It is set by custom.

c It is learned by the listener.

d The kind of music and the place where it is listened to.

5 Point 6. Which of the following is true?

a Knowing the technicalities of music is essential to one's enjoyment of it.

b Classical music always takes a while before you can enjoy it.

c You need intelligence to appreciate classical music.

d One can enjoy classical music more with a better understanding of it.

6 According to point 7, which of the following statements is/are true?

  a Impure notes can be exciting.

  b All groups are careful not to damage their instruments.

  c Some of what has been said about classical music applies to pop.

  d Anarchistic means exciting.

7 Point 8 says which of the following?

  a Image is as important to classical music as it is to pop.

  b Pop stars are pestered by the press.

  c Image is not really important to a pop group's success.

  d If pop stars get into trouble the press keeps quiet about it:

8 Point 9 says which of the following?

  a Humour during a concert is sometimes acceptable.

  b Robbie Williams has signed a contract for £80 million. What he has to do for the money is to give good performances.

  c Robbie will need to improve his singing.

  d Robbie has only just achieved fame.

9 In five sentences describe the kind of music you like, how you listen to it (for example, on CDs) and what it is that you like about the music.

10 In another five sentences say whether or not you think the music you enjoy is important. Would it make any difference if it went out of fashion and was no longer played?

11 In your own words write a definition of *aesthetic evaluation*. Then do *either* question 12 *or* question 13.

12 'Anyone can produce a piece of art.' What do you think of that statement? Try to give illustration and example in expressing you views (about 200 words).

13 Art is pointless. We can manage without it. Write about 200 words on this controversial statement, expressing your views and giving example, and illustrations.

10

The media

The main media outlets are the press, radio and television. We have next to no influence on any of them. It is sometimes difficult to decide from the newspapers what the news really is because the editors choose which items to lead on and sometimes those items are not reports of what has happened but are campaigns by editors. A selection of headlines showing news stories from eight newspapers of the same day illustrates this point about editorial selection.

The first case study points out that selling newspapers is a business – a business that depends on advertising to survive. The items that newspapers tend to push are those that they feel will encourage sales and those supporting the views of the owner of the newspaper.

Among the favourite tricks of all the media are:

- asking questions which imply their own answer;
- using gossip from a friend of someone important;
- insertion of emotive language;
- beginning with the phrase, 'usually reliable sources';
- using the opinion of the 'man in the street'.

When reading a newspaper it is always important to know who owns it and what its political persuasion is. The *Daily Mail*, for example, being a newspaper that strongly supports the Conservative Party, regularly criticizes the Labour Prime Minister, his Ministers and people related to them.

Compared with the television, radio news can be very concentrated. You are given more news for the same time than on television, but television can bring scenes of destruction and suffering right into your living-room and so arouse strong emotions. The ability of radio and television to educate us generally about the world is particularly valuable – particularly for examination courses!

The popularity of 'soaps' is dealt with as is the extent to which some people are too much involved with the plots and characters, identifying themselves with these 'persons' and generally referring to them by their role name rather than their actual name. Does this matter?

There is more about pop and high culture and how these are catered for on radio and television.

The controversial question of censorship is introduced with a brief description of how it works and its effect. The chapter concludes with a number of arguments in favour of and against censorship, with an invitation to add to them.

■ Introduction – news media

What are *the media*? The word is a plural noun for the important means of mass communication. The press, television and radio reach out to millions of people who want to be reached, for they regularly buy newspapers, listen to the radio and watch television. We boast that our press, radio and television is free from government control, a right which does not exist in all countries.

Given the definition of the term 'media' it follows that they must include the following:

- newspapers;
- television;
- radio.

Between them they do a great deal of communicating, but it does not mean that you need or would choose whatever is communicated. You have no control or influence over it, except marginally when you have a letter or email published in the press or manage to express your views on one of the various discussion programmes on radio or television, by personal appearance, 'phone-in, or by having your letter or email read out. If you disapprove of what is being featured you can refuse to buy a paper and switch off the television or radio, but the point is that you may do all these things because you do not approve of what is being communicated in principle. You may avoid sex and violence in the media because you dislike it. You are therefore free from it. However, you may still think it wrong, or even immoral, that it should feature in the organs of mass communication.

As far as the press is concerned the editor of each newspaper, influenced by its owner, decides which 'events' to push and which to suppress or minimalize. If you happened to glance at your local newsagent's paper rack on 7 December 2002 you would have seen some very different front page headlines:

Express
Asylum blamed for AIDS crisis in Britain

Financial Times
O'Neill quits as Treasury Secretary

Guardian
US slide prompts Bush purge

Independent
Russia demands return of Chechen rebel

Mail
D . . . and the baby buried in her garden

Mirror
How did you fall for him, C . . .?

Star

Asylum seekers get free massage

Sun

Heroin will kill, W . . .

(Please note: names have been omitted, but if curiosity gets the better of you try the newspapers' websites.)

What was the important news on that day? There is, of course, much more coverage inside the newspapers, but what the selection of headlines reveals is that the editors of eight different newspapers made different decisions about the news – or rather the subject – they were going to lead with the headlines that would be on display inside newsagents, supermarkets and other outlets.

analyse this

Discussion – in small groups discuss the question of different headlines and whether we get a fair presentation of the news in this country. Consider news programmes on the radio and television.

analyse this

the media

The following case study is about the media, with special emphasis on the press.

1 In this country, and throughout the world, things happen before the papers are printed. Some of those things are highly significant. Not everything can be printed so the editors have to make a choice. Two important matters affect their decision:

- the policy of the owners of the paper, as understood by the editor;

- the need to come out with an eye-catching headline that will attract attention and sell copies.

2 Producing and selling newspapers is a business and the owners and shareholders want to see increases in circulation and greater profits. In fact, it is the advertising rather than sales that keep newspapers going and companies, wishing to reach as many people as possible, will tend to place their advertisements in the popular news-papers. The broadsheets (i.e. the large-format newspapers, for example *The Times*), generally with smaller circulations, are also used because advertisers wish to reach a wide range of people.

3 Is it possible that the press tries to manipulate us by its selection or creation of news and the way it presents 'events'? The word is in quotation marks because often the press deals with non-events: things that did not happen and are unlikely to happen.

4 Here is an example of the way the media tries to manipulate us. The year 2002 was the year of the World Cup Football Competition in Japan and Korea. In April, some three months before the competition, David Beckham, the captain of the England team, had an accident. The day after this happening two items dominated the head-lines:

- the appalling tragedy of the Israeli-Palestinian conflict;

- David Beckham's broken left foot.

It may seem flippant to dwell upon Beckham's broken second metatarsal, but the case does illustrate the way in which the news media can manipulate the public. On the morning after the event the Radio 4 *Today* programme expressed surprise that the whole country had become obsessed with the England captain's injury, as if we, the listeners, had started this intensely consuming fear for Beckham's and England's plight; as if there were a huge groundswell of anxiety about the boy's shooter and the team's prospects; as if we were responsible for the *Mirror*'s and the *Sun*'s gigan-tic headlines of the day: OUR WORST NIGHTMARE.

5 The *Sun,* its front page taken up with a picture of the footballer's foot, urged its read-ers to lay their hands on the foot at noon that day to mend it. High noon! You can laugh, unless you believe in some kind of faith healing. It is amusing until you realize that such frivolity, given such space, tends to smother out what are really important events – the tabloids are good at it, but they will always argue that it is what their readers want. At first sight of that headline one would imagine that the earth were facing an imminent earthquake or a solar collision. So, did the whole country become obsessed with David's foot? If it did, the obsession began after the media ran the story. It is a regular feature of all the news media, press, radio and television to splash stories, loaded with emotive language, and then in all innocence to express surprise that the public are so excited, so anxious, so hysterical.

6 There is one thing that is important: compared with dictatorships, the media of this country are free from government control and are free to criticize the government, its policies and any member of the government. Unless they offend the Code of Prac-tice they are free to print or broadcast what they like. What is more, they have often

served the public well when they have ferreted out some scandal or drawn attention to some injustice. The media, then, have a high degree of freedom, but each newspaper selects and puts its own slant on the news, in accordance with the views of its owner. Thus we are not always presented with pure news, a clear account in literal language of what has been happening in this country and the world.

7 Free from government control, but controlled by owners, how far can the news media be trusted? It is sometimes hard to ascertain what exactly is news – what has actually happened – when even our respectable broadsheets rely upon second- or third-hand reports and gossip and present them as front-page news. Consider this example, taken from one of the broadsheets: 'A friend of someone close to the Chancellor believes that Gordon Brown thinks . . .'. What is the reality behind this statement? The reality is that this particular newspaper, is trying to make news out of nothing more than some gossip and conjecture which at best is the forming of an opinion on incomplete information and at worst is guesswork. Do readers, even readers of the broadsheets, analyse each sentence, examine each word or do they take it as fact that Gordon Brown, Chancellor of the Exchequer, expressed a thought to someone that was accurately relayed by others to the newspaper?

8 The media often make the news by their selection and presentation, rather than giving it to their readers straight. Even when it wants to deal with facts it cannot resist trying to sway our feelings or slipping in an opinion by its use of imagery or emotional appeal: 'Blair is *rocked* by the resignation of a Minister'. Notice the image? In fact the Minister was very soon replaced and if the Prime Minister was at all upset by what happened he did not show it and the public were not aware of it.

9 A favourite technique of the media is to ask a loaded question – a question that, because of the way it is presented, seems to carry its own answer. It is as if they are making a statement instead of asking a question. Here are some examples of actual questions:

- Is the Conservative Party finished as a party of government?

- Is the National Health Service crumbling under this government?

- Has sad Les outlived his usefulness for Amanda?

- Was the government's policy for dealing with foot-and-mouth a total disaster?

- Are his/her days numbered as (minister, football manager, director, etc.)?

You must often wonder who the man in the street is, whose opinions are always being sought.

10 We may find opinion interesting, and sometimes we need opinions, from all sides, especially on controversial subjects, but we need facts first. Opinion should be entirely separated from the facts. If it is opinion then it should be made clear that it is someone's opinion. In the case of the press it is generally the owner's opinion, so we all need to be aware of where the message is coming from. If you read one paper unthinkingly, you will believe that adopting the euro currency will be a disaster and if you read another unthinkingly, you will believe that not adopting it will be a disaster.

11 Be aware too that the *Mail* and the *Telegraph* are pro-Conservative and very anti-Labour, whereas the *Guardian* is pro-Labour, so you cannot expect unbiased

editorials or articles, although sometimes these newspapers will accept articles written by contributors of different political persuasions. We can live with biased editorials when we know where the opinions expressed are coming from. The danger exists in the tendency of newspapers to allow their views to infiltrate what they are presenting as news. Look out for the imagery. Look out any item that begins: 'Usually reliable sources . . .'. Not knowing the 'sources', we are unable to judge whether or not they are reliable. When reading a newspaper remember these tricks of the trade and be aware of which stable the paper comes from.

Questions

1 Point 1. Which of the following factors influence what goes into a newspaper?

   a What the owner of the newspapers think.

   b The need to make a good profit.

   c Only a.

   d Both a and b.

2 Look at point 2 and decide which of the following statements are true:

   a it is important to have a large circulation so that a large number of people can read the news;

   b advertisers tend to use the popular newspapers so that they can reach a wide range of people;

   c newspapers depend upon advertising;

   d advertisers will use popular newspapers to reach a large number of readers.

3 The use of the word 'manipulate' in point 3 suggests which of the following?

   a The press tries to please us.

   b The press tries to control us.

   c The press tries to persuade us.

   d The press tries to help us.

4 Why do you think the item about the Israeli–Palestinian conflict appears in point 4, which deals with Beckham's injury? Which of the following is the best reason?

   a It is important news.

   b It is a tragedy.

c It illustrates the fact that editors do not always choose the most serious news.

d It illustrates the fact that editorial choice is made according to what is more likely to sell newspapers, rather than what is important.

5 Point 5 explains that the media stir up the public a) with stories that are given prominence and b) by using emotive language. They then express surprise at the public's reaction. Which of the following is this an example of?

a hypocrisy;

b honesty;

c innocence;

d lying.

6 Which of the following does point 6 suggest is to the credit of the media of this country?

a that the press is free;

b that it has highlighted some bad practices;

c that it puts its own slant on the news;

d that it has acted in the cause of justice.

7 Look at point 7, the quotation beginning 'a friend of someone . . .'. It does not say what Gordon Brown said – if, in fact, he said anything at all. Which alternative, a, b, c or d, contains all and only the words which are likely to cast doubt on the story?

a Chancellor believes

b thinks friend

c friend someone close believes thinks

d friend someone close believes.

8 Consider the danger of an expression like the following: 'A friend of someone close to the Chancellor believes that Gordon Brown thinks . . .'. Which of the following options best explains what that danger is?

a Readers may take the statement as a factual report of what the Chancellor said.

b Readers may not stop to analyse the exact meaning of the statement.

c What the Chancellor thinks is not news.

d The 'someone' may have told lies.

9 According to point 9 what do the five questions have in common? Give the best answer.

a They were all asked by the media.

b They all imply or suggest that the answer is 'yes'.

c They are all short and to the point.

d They are all unfair questions.

10 After studying point 10 and 11 decide which of the following statements are true.

a Different newspapers have different views on joining the euro currency.

b The public does not want opinion; it wants facts.

c Sometimes editorial opinion is included in the presentation of news.

d Editorials are unbiased.

11 Which of the following best describes the general argument of this case study?

a Do not trust the press.

b Do not trust the media.

c We have to be careful that the media does not manipulate us.

d Often the needs of each newspaper come before our need for news.

12 From the case study 1 pick out three examples of fact and three examples which are opinion, or which imply an opinion. Then write out the relevant parts.

13 Bearing in mind the main points in the case study give a presentation in which you compare several different newspapers of the same date. It will be useful to photocopy some items for your audience. You will find this very interesting and here are a few suggestions to start you off.

● Look for the use of imagery in news reporting which expresses a viewpoint.

● Compare different treatments of the same news story.

● Examine different news items which each paper highlights.

■ Radio and television

In both these media listeners or viewers can be influenced by emotive language used to capture their interest and maintain their loyalty to the station or channel. The competition is not of the same order as that between newspapers because the BBC does not rely upon advertising revenue (although independent television does). The public pays for the BBC through the annual licence. Independent television needs good viewing figures to attract advertising revenue, which pays for programmes. Nonetheless there is competition between the different corporations for audience ratings the BBC wants to be seen to be doing better than ITV. This rivalry means that there is a tendency to try to make the news interesting – perhaps more interesting than the bare news itself warrants. As it is television news, programmes have to be accompanied by pictures, some of which are essential to convey fully what has happened (for example starvation in Africa) and some of which are interesting (such as the arrival at one of our airports of a 'star' of the pop or film world).

What is particularly important about television coverage of the news is that some footage, such as war scenes, disasters and all types of human suffering, affect the viewers emotionally much more than press reports. It is common, therefore, for viewers to be warned when something distressing is about to be shown. Radio news, on the other hand, not having pictures, often gives a more concentrated news package. You can get more news on the radio than you would for the same time on television, depending upon which radio station you tune into.

Education

Radio and television are very informative and present programmes on all kinds of subjects: religion, morality, culture, art, politics, economics and more. Television can take you to places you have not been and help you to understand something of their culture. Radio and television both carry specific education programmes: for example the BBC presents Open University degree courses and *Byte-Size* revision courses for GCSE. It is possible that the latter have made some contribution to improving examination results. Independent television, satellite and cable also have their quota of educational and cultural programmes. Sky, for example, provides specific programmes on history and geography.

Entertainment

During the daytime there are regular and frequent quizzes, cookery and antiques programmes, presentational programmes and old films. There is a wide variety of comedy, drama, soap serials, film and popular music programmes. As you have already seen, Sky has quite a few pop music channels. Radio is not without its entertainment, offering a similar menu, apart from film. Like TV it has some very popular and long-running programmes, for example, *Desert Island Discs, Just a Minute, I'm Sorry I Haven't a Clue* and the ever-popular soap, *The Archers*. It could be argued that it has remained quite successful in its own field despite the more glamorous television, although car radios and portable radios have contributed to this success.

Behind the scenes

What radio and television shows have in common is that they are seldom broadcast cold, without any kind of rehearsal. Studio audiences are in a sense behind the scenes, for they can witness any errors and how they are dealt with.

I was once in the audience of a quiz show in which there were three contestants and an actor as quiz master. All went well until the question was asked: 'Which actor was in the *Blues Brothers* who also appeared in the film *Curly Sue?*' Contestant A answered 'Dan Ackroyd' and contestant B answered 'John Belushi'. Contestant B was judged right and given the point. During a break, Contestant A told the quiz master that the answer could not have been John Belushie because he had died before *Curly Sue* was in production. A technician agreed and said that it was James Belushie, John's brother. As the quiz was a Trivial Pursuits game and each contestant had been filmed with a number of pieces on his Trivia board, the scores could not be altered without ruining continuity so it was agreed that the old question would be cut and a new question inserted in place of the original question.

The new question was, 'Who played Jake in the *Blues Brothers?*' to which the answer was 'John'. So Contestant B's score and the number of Trivial Pursuits pieces were kept intact.

Contestant A was compensated for having been asked a false question. So when it came to a first-on-the-buzzer question Contestant A was allowed to press first, the other two contestants, holding back their fingers, pretending not to know the answer. Incidentally Contestant C won the holiday for two in Amsterdam.

The above has been described in detail so that you will know how things are done behind the scenes. The programmes come out smoothly, without any interruption, and for that we must thank those responsible for continuity. In filming, whenever there is a mistake, the corrections are made, but there is no audience. What the audience sees is the perfect finish.

Soaps

These cannot be ignored for they are a special feature of radio (*The Archers*) and a regular speciality of television. How many decades has *Coronation Street* been running? What is 'soap'? The term 'soap opera' was first coined in America in the 1930s to describe long-running, family programmes on radio, which were sponsored in the main by soap companies. A feature of those programmes on radio was that they seemed to go on and each episode ended leaving listeners in suspense, wondering what would happen next. Listeners became hooked on them. Does this sound familiar? Like the people in *Coronation Street,* the inhabitants of Walford, the fictional suburb in *Eastenders,* go through some quite traumatic experiences. What is so special about these programmes is that many viewers of television and listeners to radio soaps become so emotionally involved, and identify so closely with particular characters that they almost delude themselves into seeing their programme as reality and the characters as real persons They send 'get well' cards to any character who has to act being ill and threatening letters to the villains, especially to any 'person' who treats badly, or 'cheats' on, the viewer's favourite character. There have even been cases where fictional doctors have been written to by the public asking for their advice! Does it matter?

analyse this

Write about 300 words on the phenomenon where listeners and viewers treat their favourite soap as if it were real. You may like to consider the following points:

- How did this start?

- Is this a case of entertainment that has gone too far?

- Are creators of the plots and the directors responsible?

- Is it just a bit of harmless fun?

- Do those who so overreact suffer from some psychological condition?

- Should such programmes be banned as harmful because they cause some people to suffer from delusions?

Soaps are something that the press wants to get in on and what they do is to reveal the plots in the coming week's programmes. The *Daily Mirror* of 3 December 2002 showed pictures of scenes from the Christmas programmes of *Eastenders* also revealing:

- who realizes that he couldn't be the father of his wife's expected baby;

- who returns to the programme;

- who are in a love triangle;

- who dies and who knocked him down.

But he's already married to me!

Don't miss tomorrow night's episode!

analyse
this

Ien Ang considers this phenomenon in Corner and Hawthorn's 1993 book *Communication Studies*:

> *How do viewers get involved in a television serial like* Dallas, *and what does this involvement consist of? The Belgian media theoretician Jean-Marie Piemme, in his book on the television serial genre, asserts that this involvement occurs because viewers are enabled to participate in the 'world' of the serial. This participation does not come of its own accord, but must be* produced:

> *If, in the serial . . . participation can be brought about, this is certainly because this activity has psychological foundations, but it is also because these psychological foundations are confronted by a type of discourse allowing them to be activated. In other words, the structure of the discourse which sustains the serial produces the participation as well as the psychological attitude.*

> *The structure of the text itself therefore plays an essential role in stimulating the involvement of viewers. More importantly still, according to Piemme, it is impossible to watch a television serial without some degree of personal involvement. 'To watch a serial', he states, 'is much more than seeing it: it is also involving oneself in it, letting oneself be held in suspense, sharing the feelings of the characters, discussing their psychological motivations and their conduct, deciding whether they are right or wrong, in other words living "their world,"' but what is there so particular about the textual structure of television serials that makes them able to effect such profound involvement?*

It has already been mentioned that viewers or listeners identify with a particular character. But there is no interaction between the viewer/listener and the character. So how does the viewer/listener comprehend the character's personality. Ien Ang further explains:

One does not just recognize oneself in the ascribed characteristics of an isolated fictional character. That character occupies a specific position within the context of the narrative as a whole: only in relation to other characters in the narrative is her or his 'personality' brought out. In other words identification with a character only becomes possible within the framework of the whole structure of the narrative.

A realistic performance is essential: 'the "lifelike" acting style ensures that the distance between actor and character is minimalized, so that the illusion is created that we are dealing with a "real person".'

If you watch soaps, write about any of the characters you identify with or whose role and performance you enjoy. Write about 300 words explaining what it is about this character that you appreciate and how he or she enters into the role and gives a believable performance. If you do not watch soaps, pick a character from any programme, video, film or stage play you have seen and do the same.

■ Pop and high culture

Chapter 6 has considered pop and high culture and Chapter 8 introduced the science and art of DJ-ing. It would seem reasonable for people to take an interest in all kinds of music but in the end it is a matter of choice and a question of whether the broadcasting media caters for all taste. It is easier to survey the radio to consider this question. The following seems to apply:

- Radio 1 and independent radio cater for pop culture.
- Radio 2 caters for popular tastes, more comprehensive.
- Radio 3 caters for high culture.
- Classic FM caters for high culture to light popular.
- Radio 4 caters for news, serious, comedy, variety, drama.
- Local radio (BBC) – as for Radio 4, but the emphasis is on local affairs.
- Radio 5 has sport, news and 'phone-ins'.

analyse this

Conduct a group investigation and report back. Obtain some copies of a programme publication, for example *TV Times*. Working in pairs, each group should study a different station's programmes for a week – three days, if time is pressing – and each group should do a presentation on the types of programme discovered. Are there any changes that groups would make to the list given above? When all the presentations have been made are there any conclusions about the balance of programmes between the stations? Are all tastes catered for?

Each terrestrial TV channel carries its own variety of programmes, although BBC 2 carries more high-culture programmes. Satellite and cable cater for a wide range of interests. They have many music channels, a history channel and a drama channel, although some of the channels have to be paid for separately.

■ Censorship

The BBC is under the control and administration of a board of appointed governors and in the last analysis it is answerable to Parliament. The Independent Broadcasting Authority is responsible for regulating independent radio and televisions stations and for selling advertising to private companies. Local companies have been set up to carry out the IBA's policy in the regions. Both these bodies have overall responsibility for what appears on TV and radio.

The British Board of Film Classification has a set of guidelines and awards age categories to films and videos: 18, 15, 12 and U. It can refuse to grant a certificate to films or videos or cut out parts of them. According to its website it draws a distinction between what it calls 'manners' – flexible public attitudes on, for example, nudity, and obscene language – and morals – unchanging codes of conduct. It is guided by the Obscene Publications Act, 1959 which prohibits anything which may deprave or corrupt persons who are likely to read, see or listen to such material. The BBFC is answerable to the Department of Culture, Media and Sport. On top of this, local authorities have the power to refuse permission to allow any cinema in their area to show any film.

analyse this

the film censor

The following case study is taken from the *Independent on Sunday,* 21 July 2002. The article is about the retirement of Andreas Whittam Smith, the President of the British Board of Film Classification after over four years in the post. The following is a series of extracts from the article, which begins by explaining in the president's own words how he can get on with makers of pornographic films:

'When these sex film people sent a delegation to our offices, I said to them: "This Office Tart *movie* – it's got no artistic merit whatsoever, has it?" They replied: "No." I said: "It's not meant for anything other than sheer titillation, is it?" They replied: "No, that's right."

'I immediately thought to myself, "I can work with these people." "What I liked about them is that they had absolutely no cant,' he explains. 'That seemed so refreshing."

Branded the X-rated censor . . . his tenure has been attended by countless controversies. With his approval, the board belatedly approved the release of a slew [large number] of 'video nasties', from The Texas Chainsaw Massacre *to* Straw Dogs.

Films containing full-frontal nudity and all manner of amorous activities now qualify for 15 certificates . . . At the same time, the board has signalled its intention to downgrade the 12 classification to 'advisory-only'.

Yet it has been far from a free-for-all. For every relaxation, there has been a subtle tightening of the rules at the margins. References to drugs have been all but eradicated from movies with anything less than an 18 certificate, while graphic sexual violence remains virtually taboo.

[The retiring president] is hardly your typical subversive. The son of a Merseyside clergyman, he was for many years business editor of the Daily Telegraph.

There's one mystery I've never been able to fathom the whole time I've been in this job, which is why the British allow themselves to be the most regulated nation in the world . . . Is it because we are more puritanical? No that doesn't wash because the United States is very puritanical in some ways, but far less heavily regulated . . . To me, the BBFC's primary job should simply be to enable parents to regulate their children's viewing.

Though it may seem odd for the nation's supreme arbiter of taste and decency to disapprove of censorship, Mr Whittam Smith is confident he speaks for the majority of the British public.

He retires as president of the BBFC to work for the Church of England as Estates Commissioner.

'I've now swapped the company of pornographers for the company of bishops. At the age of 65, that's probably not such a bad thing.'

Questions

1 How was it that the President of the BBFC could get on with the makers of pornographic films?

2 Did he have a smooth run as censor, without any disagreements? Give reasons for your answer.

3 Looking at his career and what he says, do you think that he wanted to ban censorship and let the media produce whatever it wishes? Give reasons for your answer.

4 Does Mr Whittam Smith think that he is a lone voice or does he believe that he has support for his ideas on censorship? Give reasons for answer.

5 Explain in your own words what he means by the very last sentence.

Questions 1 to 5 can be answered by reading the case study. The next question is one of opinion.

6 From what you have read, write about 150 words on whether you think that he was a good censor, someone who served the film-going, video-watching public well. Look for evidence from what is said and what is implied.

key terms

cant

Talk of morality which is not genuine.

subversive

Someone who tries to overthrow the government or undermine morality.

key terms

ayatollah

Shiite religious leader.

fatwa

In Muslim countries, a religious ruling or command.

shiite

Member of one of the two main branches of Islam (pronounced *shee-ite*).

It sometimes seems to be ignored, but there is a voluntary agreement under which only TV programmes of a family nature will be shown up to 9 p.m. – 'the watershed'.

Another restriction is that anyone publishing or broadcasting that which tends to damage a person's character without any justification for doing so can be sued for damages under the Defamation Act 1996.

The obscenity and defamation laws apply to all the media, including the stage. Different religions have different degrees of tolerance and what might pass censorship in this country may not do so in other countries. Many Christians in this country objected to the film *The Life of Brian*, which was a kind of comic and absurd parallel to the life of Christ, including a crucifixion, with those on the crosses singing *Always Look on the Bright Side of Life*. Blasphemy against Christianity is a criminal offence, but hardly anyone is prosecuted under it. 'When it was first published, Muslims objected to Salman Rushdie's book, *The Satanic Verses*, because they thought it sacrilegious (attacking sacred beliefs). Most Muslim states banned the book and, indeed, there were instances where it was ceremonially burned. A *fatwa* was placed on the author's life by the Iranian Ayatollah, which urged Muslims to rise up and kill the author. For years Rushdie had to have police protection, but the threat seems to have eased off, partly because the Ayatollah has since died and partly because the Iranian government has said that it would not encourage anyone to harm Rushdie. However, the government and the Muslim clerics did not quite see eye to eye and technically the *fatwa* is still in force.

Remember, from Chapter 6, that D.H. Lawrence's novel, *Lady Chaterley's Lover*, was banned for many years, as were his paintings, but it is rare for such bans to be imposed nowadays.

Internet

What appears on the internet is very difficult to control. There have been incidents of defamation of character, of different types of obscene sites, including attempts by paedophiles to contact and seduce under age people . Tracking down offenders often needs a joint international effort, but rings of paedophiles from a number of countries have been arrested.

Modern computers and television have a facility that allows parents to control what is seen on the screen, but it is not possible to exclude all programmes that parents would not wish their children to see.

Should there be censorship? Should works of art be banned?

Reasons for

- Some material is highly sensitive and it could be detrimental to the security of the state.

- Some material may be so depraved that it may corrupt people and weaken the moral fibre of the country.

- An important influence on what people become – their personality, attitudes and behaviour – is their social experience, so it follows that morally corrupt programmes are likely to corrupt the viewers.

Reasons against

- In a democracy people need the facts to be able to understand and to make reasoned and responsible choices.

- It should be for adults to judge where any material is likely to deprave them, and what exactly is the country's moral fibre.

- There is no evidence to show that people are more influenced by obscenity and depravity than their experiences of morality and enlightenment.

- The last film censor, Whittam Smith, does not seem to have been affected by his job.

analyse this

In groups, discuss these reasons for and against censorship and think up another three or more arguments for and against censorship. Then write about 300 words on the subject, using what you read in this chapter. Explain clearly the important arguments for and against and express your own thought-out point of view.

■ A short whole-book quiz

1 Name three of the universal rights.

2 What is the difference between assisted suicide and euthanasia?

3 What is an atheist?

4 What philosophical approach did Jeremy Bentham put forward?

5   Which religion did Julius Caesar come across when he invaded Britain?

6   Which religion does not include a belief in God?

7   Which religious groups worship in:

   a a mosque

   b a synagogue?

8   What is polytheism?

9   Explain reincarnation.

10 What is a faith school?

11 What is the meaning of *Acculturation?*

12 In dictatorships what purpose do the arts normally have to serve?

13 What is didactic art?

14 What is meant by the expression 'artists and the interrelationship with their audience'?

15 What and where is the Parthenon?

16 Is the following statement true: 'Gothic churches have rounded windows and doors'?

17 Name two Renaissance painters.

18 Give an example of a pop-artist painter.

19 What is meant by '*high culture*'?

20 What is the definition of a 'soap' programme?

■ End piece

'I find television very educating. Every time somebody turns on the set I go into the other room and read a book.' (Groucho Marx)

index

Page numbers in **bold** indicate where the term has been defined in the text

abortion 50, 51
acculturation **58**
action painting 113, **115**
aesthetic evaluation 118–20
Afrikaners **22**
Animal Farm 90
art nouveau 113, **105**
art, abstract 113, **115**; beauty and 109; Christian 84; conceptual 91, 113, **116**; didactic 84–8; exhibitions 98–9; Indo-Islamic 112, **114**; modern 90, 113; pop 107–8, 113, **115**; timeline 111–16
artists 80–108; and history 88–9; audiences and 95–108; creative role of 81–2; in democracies 81; in dictatorships 81; purpose of 82–84; role 90–2
Arts Council of England survey 95–7
arts, in education 103–104; participation in 100
ascetic **44**
atheist 21
atone **41**
audiences 95–108
awe **37**
ayatollah **141**

Bach, J.S. 85
ballet 121

Baroque 112, **114**; music 120
Bayeaux Tapestry 88, 112
beauty 109, 118
Beethoven, L. van 115, 116, 120
belief 1, 3–4, 28
Bentham, J. 23
Billington, R. 19, 21–2
Bosch, H. 109
Brahma **38**
Bronte, C. 90
Buddha **43**
Buddhism 27, 35, 37, 38, 43–4, 51
Butler, J. 91

Canaletto 86
cant **141**
capital punishment 10
capitalism **25**
Catholicism 6, 45, 51
censorship 126, 139–42
Chiswick House 111, 113
Christianity 37, 38, 41
Christians 31
circumcision **40**
Classical art 112; music 120
clubbing 101, 121
concerts, rock and pop 98
conformity 47–50
conscience 7–8
conservatism 25

contraception 50, 51
Cubism 113, **115**
culture 52–79
culture, American 63; Asian and Australian 74–6; British 56–7; changes in 68; high 52, 54, 76–7, 126, 138–9; Jewish 59–60; language and 52, 63–7; national 55; popular ('pop') 52, 54, 77–8, 126, 138–9; science, technology and 56; sex and 53, 67

Dali, S. 110, 113, 115, 118
dharma 35, 36, **43**
didacticism **88**
dilemmas, moral **1,** 5–6, 47
disjointed interaction **95**
Druidism 31
Duchamp, M. 83

Elsen, A. 84
Emin, T. 92, 113, 116, 118
empiricism **1**
Englishness 62
eruv **59**
essay-type answers, advice 17
euthanasia **13**
Expressionism 109, **115**

faith **28**

145

fatwa **142**
Fighting Téméraire, The 110, 113, 115
film 97, 98, 99
film censor 139
Five Pillars of Islam 42
Four Noble Truths **44**
fundamentalism 59

Gautama 43, 44
Giotto 112, 119
Gombrich, E. 104
Gothic architecture 112, **114**
Guernica 89, 91, 119

Handel, G. 85
Hebrew **40, 60**
Hinduism 37, 38, 39, 42–3
Hirst, D. 84
Hitler, A. 36
homosexuality 14, 50, 67

immigrants 57–8
impressionism **105–6,** 113, **115**
induction 2
inductive learning **54**
interaction 95, **97**
Internet 141
Islam 31, 37, 38, 39, 42

Jehova's Witnesses 47
Judaism 37, 38, 40

karma 43

Lady Chatterley's Lover 66
laity 36
language 4, 63–7
law 8, 14–15, 28–30
Lawrence, D.H. 66
Lichtenstein, R. 108

media 125–43; news 126–31; tricks of 125
Medieval art 112, **114**
Messiah **40**
Michelangelo 76, 85
Mill, J.S.. 23
moksha 43
Mona Lisa, The 82, 110, 112, 114, 119
Mondrian, P. 110
monotheistic **41**
Moorish art 112, **114**
morality 4; changes in 50–1; codes 9–10, 14, 16, 47; definition **9**; dilemmas **1**, 5–6, 47; education and 50–1; law and 8, 14; principles 6; religion and 19–20, 45–51; variation between individuals

15–16; variation between societies 10
motor neurone disease **12**
Mozart, W. 120
Munch, E. 110, 113, 115
music 99, 120–22
musicals 97

National Curriculum 46, 103
news 125–31
Nirvana **44**
Noble Eight-fold Path **44**
Norman architecture 112, **114**
novels 99

Old Testament 40
opera 121
orthodox **40**
Orwell, G. 90
Owen, W. 118

painting 99
Pali Canon (Tipitaka) **38**
Palladian 108, **114**
Palladio, A. 111, 114
pantomime 98
paradox **41**
Parthenon 110, 112, 114
performing 102–103
Picasso 89, 90, 119
plays 97, 98
poetry 99
Pollock, J. 115
Popper, K. 2
Post-Impressionism 113, **115**
Pre-Raphaelite 109, **115**
profane **37**

Qur'an 42

radio 134–6, 138–9; news 126
rationalism **2**, 3
Read, H. 84
reincarnation **30, 43,** 44
religion, ancient and modern 31; atheism and 21–2; concepts associated with 27–30; faith 28; moral influence of 19–20, 28; origins 30
religions, checklist 38–9; comparison 38–40; major 37–44; statistics 38
religious and moral education 45–51
Rembrandt 85, 112
Renaissance 111, 112, **114,** 119
Renoir, P. 110
resurrection **41**
Rococo 112, **114**
Romantic, music 120

Romanticism 113, **115,** 120

sabbath **40**
salvation **41**
sanctioned **37**
schools 48–9; Catholic 45; faith 45–6
Scream, The 110, 113, 115
sculpture 99
shariah **10, 42**
Shaw, G.B. 47–8, 90
shiite **141**
Sikhism 39
Sistine Chapel 80
small-group discussion, advice 17
soaps 126, 135–8
socialism **25**
standards 15
Steen, J. 86
subcultures 57–9
subversive **141**
suicide **13,** assisted **13**
Surrealism 113, **115**
Sydney Opera House 110, 115–16
syllogism **3, 4**

Tate Gallery 90, 91
technology 56
television 134–9, 142
Ten Commandments, The 20, 29, 40
theatre 97, 98
thinking, ways of 65–6
Tipitaka (Pali Canon) **38**
Titian 112, 119
tolerance 32–6
Trinity, The **38**
truth 1
Turner Prize 81, 90, 116
Turner, J. 110, 113, 115

Universal Declaration of Human Rights 11
utilitarianism 22–5

values 9–10
Van Gogh, V. 110, 113, 115
Vermeer, J. 88, 110, 112
Vinci, L. da 86, 110, 112, 119
Vivaldi, A. 114

Wagner, R. 81
Warhol, A. 107–8
Wilde, O. 14
Wilton Diptych 85, 112, 114

Yiddish **60**
Young V. 102–103